Welcome to the Weirdness

America. It's the land of white picket fences, of rationally planned grid-based city blocks, of organised and wholesome normality, right? Wrong. The United States is possibly the weirdest nation on Earth.

Where else would aliens visit apart from the only superpower on the planet? The USA's vast wealth and military prowess mean that it's packed with secrets that humans and extraterrestrials alike would like to uncover. Meanwhile, its dense forests, broad plains, bizarre badlands and trackless mountains are rumoured to be home to denizens neither human nor animal, neither settler or Native. Here Bigfoot and other more fearsome creatures are reputed to lurk, while others like Mothman are believed to creep into the shadows of small towns and suburbia, portentiously skirting the edgelands of human habitation for purposes unknown.

But even the cities and the people who live in them have their fair share of the strange. From architectural advice beyond the grave to arcane symbols and mysterious methods of construction, even the most ordinary American street can hide the most uncanny of secrets. Come with us now on a trip to discover just some of them...

CONTENTS

CROSS THE STATES ON A...
Ghost-to-Ghost ROAD TRIP
10

06 *Home of the Strange*
Welcome to the weird side of America

10 *Ghost to Ghost Road Trip*
East Coast to West in search of haunts and horrors

26 *Weird Washington D.C.*
The capital city of strange

30 *Formed in the USA*
The USA's weirdest natural wonders

40 *The Mysterious Marfa Lights*
The inexplicable orbs that haunt a Texas town

42 *New Orleans: Voodoo-Vibed Necropolis*
America's most haunted city

46 *Bad but Beautiful*
The bizarre landscapes of America's badlands

52 *The Stilt Village of Ukivok*
An Alaskan village with a difference

54 *If You Go Down to the Woods*
What haunts the forests of Portlock, Alaska?

56 *Road to Nowhere: US-83 Highway*
This open road is all there is for miles

60 *Elkmont's Synchronised Fireflies*
These Tennessee bugs put on an unusual show

62 *The Mystery of Roanoke*
What happened to this early European colony?

66 *Peculiar Peninsulas & Idiosyncratic Islands*
Remote islands and tiny places

Contents

IT'S OUT OF THIS WORLD!
Over 100 PLACES TO VISIT!
DESERT DAY TRIPS TO ROSWELL
120

94

106

62

112

42

---

74 *Overseas Highway: Florida Keys*
A drive with a difference through Florida's isles

76 *The Building of Coral Castle*
How did one man create these strange structures?

78 *New York City of Weird*
The Big Apple's most bonkers places

82 *The Headless Horseman's Haunt*
Sleepy Hollow and the making of a myth

84 *Strange Attractions*
Tourist hotspots with a distinct difference

92 *The Lost Sea*
A mysterious underground world awaits

94 *Strange San Francisco*
Frisco's freakiest locations

98 *The Bridgewater Triangle*
A Massachusetts mystery

100 *Eerie Appalachia*
Home of monsters and magic

106 *Carhenge*
America's answer to Stonehenge

108 *La La Land Los Angeles*
Putting the Hollyweird in Tinsel Town

112 *The Fremont Troll*
Seattle's bridge guardian

114 *The Loneliest Road in America*
Nevada's isolated Route 50

118 *Fire Down Below*
Centralia has been burning for deccades

120 *What Really Happened in Roswell?*
Did aliens crash-land in New Mexico?

124 *Area 51*
State secrets in the Nevada desert

05

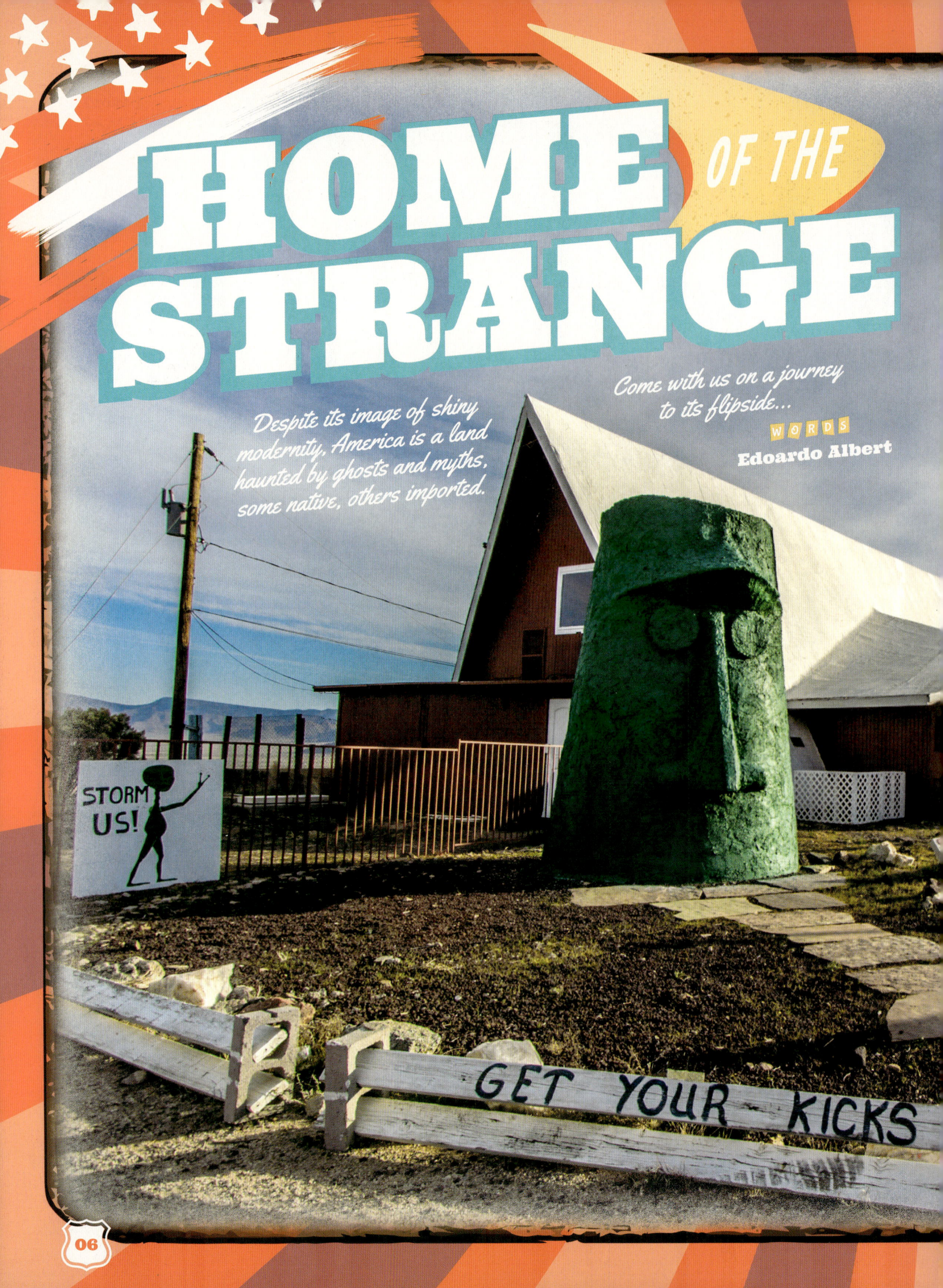

HOME OF THE STRANGE

Despite its image of shiny modernity, America is a land haunted by ghosts and myths, some native, others imported. Come with us on a journey to its flipside...

WORDS Edoardo Albert

Home of the Strange

It's not a melting pot on the shadow side. There, in the places where strange beliefs and stranger phenomena meet and mingle, America is a place where the ghosts and spirits that walked the forests and prairies before the arrival of Europeans met and mingled with the stories of witches and ghouls that the settlers brought with them. Rather than melting into a homogenous mass, the beliefs and ideas of Native Americans and European settlers fed into each other, bringing new and unique ideas and phenomena to birth.

America was where Bigfoot walked under the trees and flying saucers buzzed through the sky. It was - it is - a place where old beliefs collided with the spirit of progress, bringing things entirely new into this world. Starting with the American obsession with the automobile, then leaping into the sky (and beyond) with the invention of the aeroplane, America is where urban legends of strange hitchhikers and ordinary people being abducted by aliens were first whispered - and then set in six-inch newstype as lurid headlines on tabloid newspapers.

In this book we will journey across weird America, revisiting the old stories and detouring to find out about new legends. For if America is the land where people go to reinvent themselves, it's also the place where what is weird gets weirder. Time to cross the frontier of the normal and venture into the Great Wide Open.

Bringing the Old World to the New World

The first waves of European settlers to arrive in North America differed in many respects. There were the Puritans who founded the New England colonies, the Anglicans who established the Jamestown colony in Virginia, and the Dutch who founded New Amsterdam (which would later become New York). But while they differed in language and religion, they were united in two areas: they brought old names from home to their new home in the west, and they all accepted without question that the world was an arena in which God and the devil contested for the souls of men and women.

For the Puritans of New England, this contest came into sharp focus in the wiles of witches. Driven by their Calvinist theology, these settlers saw God's will as the sole cause of all events; it was their task to divine the meaning in these events. There were no accidents in their world, only more or less obscure clues as to what God wanted of them. But contesting with God was the devil and although his efforts would, they believed, ultimately be futile, yet he might employ agents in his attempts to thwart God's will. These agents were witches. It's therefore no surprise that the most notorious witch trials in American history took place in Salem, slap-bang in the middle of Puritan America.

It's all in the stars

While the Puritans of New England were obsessed with witches and portents, the Anglicans of the Virginia colony worried about the play of fortune in men's lives – and it was mostly men's lives, as their women were supposed to tend the hearth rather than take public office. As such, they studied the position of the planets and stars to learn, through astrology, when the heavens might align in their favour. In like manner, omens were signs God sent to guide men's actions: failure to read them meant you accrued the blame for whatever ill-fortune followed.

Nowhere were these signs, in the heavens and on the earth, followed more closely than in Virginia's gambling halls. The gentlemen planters of Virginia came to believe fervently that, if they read these signs aright and played when the stars were in their favour, then they could walk away from the gaming table at the end of the night much richer than when they sat down in the evening.

Into the Great Wide Open

For these early settlers, life was precarious. One colony, Roanoke, had disappeared entirely, its loss making for the first major local experience of one of the fundamental shadow stories: the lost. The disappearance of individuals or even large groups of people were common themes in European folklore, their disappearance ascribed to following the Fair Folk into their halls under hill or the lure of the piper spiriting away Hamelin's children.

In this New World, where vast, impenetrable forests stretched into an unknown distance, it was all too easy for people to disappear, willingly or unwillingly. Unlike most of Europe, there were animals in those woods that might easily take a human as prey. But then there were also other humans who moved through those woods, people who inspired wonder and dread in the settlers. European settlers hung two stereotypes around the necks of the Native Americans who moved at the edges of their settlements and on the margins of their consciences: they were both the noble savage and the savage barbarian.

The noble savage idea came first but the friction of frequent contact led to the savage barbarian trope growing among the European settlers, a stereotype that became a conviction following the massacre of 1622 in Virginia, when Chief Opechancanough, leader of the Powhatan Confederacy, led a surprise attack on the colonists, killing 437 of them. Chief Opechancanough had ordered his men to be friendly and hospitable to the colonists in the weeks before the attack so that they might drop their defences.

Abductions, kidnappings and quiet murders were all features of the conflict between the colonists and the Native Americans. People disappeared, never to be heard from again. In such a context, it's not surprising that the disappeared figure large in the weird margins of American history and American life.

> ❝ *In this New World, it was all too easy for people to disappear, willingly or unwillingly* ❞

PARANORMAL EVENTS ARE OFTEN REFERRED TO AS "FORTEAN PHENOMENA" IN HONOUR OF PIONEERING AMERICAN RESEARCHER CHARLES FORT.

Home of the Strange

Haunted forests, mysterious plains

The first colonies were tiny settlements on the fringes of a vast, unknown continent. It was only at the end of the 19th century that most of America was properly mapped: for two and a half centuries, the interior was mostly a cartographical blank where people could project their fears and their fancies.

This played out in the pioneer mentality, with its mixture of romantic adventuring and ruthless avarice, that slowly opened up the interior. The woodsmen who set off into the vast forests of the Appalachians were mostly descendants of Scottish, Irish and northern English settlers. They took with them their native superstitions of kelpies, banshees and boggarts and, under the endless canopy and on the vast buffalo plain, these figures met their Native American counterparts: the wendigo and the skin-walker, the bakwas and the great horned serpent. Primed by their own beliefs, the European frontiersmen of the 17th and 18th centuries had little difficulty accepting into their own tales the stories of the Native Americans that they traded with, defrauded, befriended and fought and, occasionally, married.

Modern myths

But America as the land of the weird was not tied to its past. If it had been, then the mapping of the continent would have slowly brought an end to the shadow tales. In fact, quite the opposite happened. When America became the skyscrapered, automobile-driving landscape of the future in the first half of the 20th century, the very instruments of its modernity became vehicles for new strands of shadow stories. The shock of the new brought in its wake urban legends of vanishing hitchhikers, UFOs and the sinister government cover-ups associated with them, and a cavalcade of paranormal events.

New myths and superstitions generally arise among dislocated people. With the vast numbers who poured into America during the 20th century, many with nothing but the clothes they stood up in, faced with a country that bore little relation to their dreams, there was fertile ground for new strands of myth making. Perhaps the most fertile areas have been where conspiracy theories meet modern myths, such as the Roswell Incident. For shadow stories are a way of fitting the wild chances of the world into some sort of comprehensible framework. The shadow stories we tell ourselves are our attempt to encompass the weird of this world and the worlds beyond.

Come with us now as we embark on a journey across this vast land of wonders, where the weird, the strange, the miraculous and the mundane can all feature on a single road trip. ★

Top left Both the witch trials in Salem and the later revulsion against them were crucial in establishing American responses to perceived internal threats to order

Above Alien and UFO belief is rife in modern America

Below left Who knows what might travel the lonely backcountry roads?

Top right Driven by curiosity (and the need to escape an abusive father) Charles Fort left home at 18 and hitchhiked around the world so that he could 'put some capital in the bank of experience'

Below Anything might lurk in a forest as endless as this

CHARLES FORT'S LONELY WORK

Through most of the 1920s, visitors to the Reading Room of the British Library would have seen a tall, stocky man with glasses and a drooping walrus moustache going through piles of scientific journals and newspapers, taking careful notes. His name was Charles Fort. He was an American and, with his wife Anna, he had left a life of poverty in the Bronx to pursue his research. Fort was studying phenomena that no one else was interested in, phenomena that would come to be named after him. He was searching for the inexplicable and the strange. The sort of phenomena that might rate half a column in a provincial newspaper and then be forgotten – unless someone made a note of it. That was what Fort was doing. Falls of fish, reports of spontaneous human combustion, unexplained disappearances, strange objects in the sky, poltergeist activity; the whole gamut of paranormal phenomena that the sciences of his day dismissed and ignored. Fort collected his work into four books, still in print today, and his spirit of irreverent scepticism animated his work with a particular humour that continues among those who follow in his footsteps. Fort made no real attempt to explain what he recorded for, in his heart, he believed that the world was not merely stranger than we imagine, but that it is stranger than we *can* imagine.

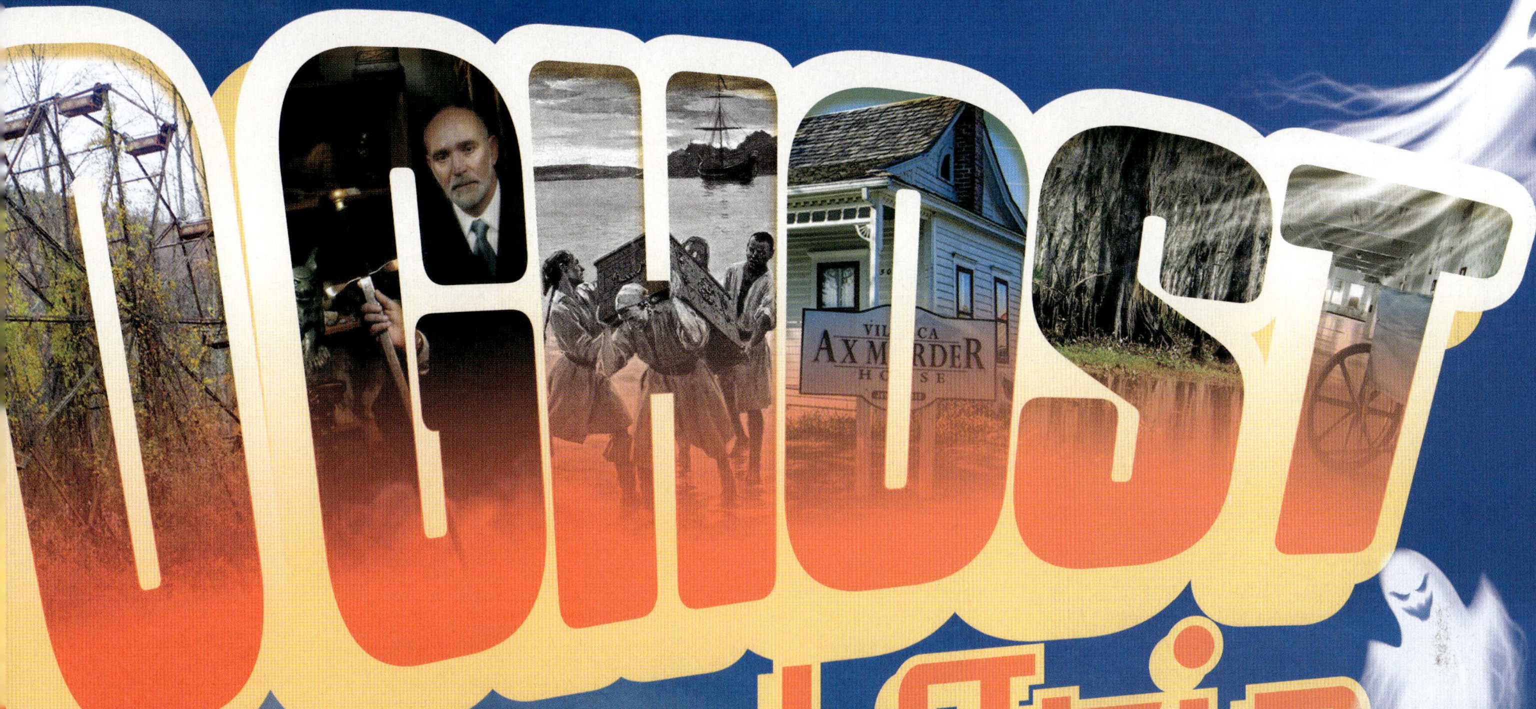

Ghost to Ghost Road Trip

GHOST Road Trip

Get your motor running with this hair-raising cross-continental journey across the USA from sea to spooky sea

WORDS April Madden & Alice Pattillo

Buckle up and prepare for the ride of a lifetime as we take a transcontinental tour of some of the USA's creepiest haunts. Starting in the northeast in Massachusetts we'll meander down the Eastern Seaboard (taking the occasional detour as we go) all the way to Florida, before heading west inland and swinging slowly northwards once more, finally reaching the West Coast and making our way south again through California. On the way we'll visit the homes of ghosts, ghouls, witches, cryptids, aliens and demons who all have one thing in common – none of them rest quietly in death.

11

'The Conjuring' House
HARRISVILLE, RHODE ISLAND
UTC-5

Known to locals and to the Perron family that lived there as the Old Arnold Estate, this farmhouse dates back to around 1736. It's the inspiration for *The Conjuring*, the first movie in the franchise of the same name, which is inspired by hauntings and demonic possessions investigated by mediums Ed and Lorraine Warren. After experiencing unsettling paranormal events during the 1970s, the Perron family called the Warrens in to investigate. The Warrens claimed they discovered a horde of unquiet spirits, the worst of which was the ghost of former resident Bathsheba Sherman, whose gravestone dated 1812-1885 (not the movie's 1849) can be found in nearby Harrisville. Legend now paints Bathsheba as an evil witch who murdered babies with pins. Whatever the historical veracity of the allegations, The Conjuring House now leans into its horror story with tours and ghost hunter-led investigations, including overnight events. It has a strict bookings-only policy.

Lizzie Borden House
FALL RIVER, MASSACHUSETTS
UTC-5

At the end of the 19th century, all was not well in the Borden household in Fall River, Massachusetts. Wealthy but frugal widower Andrew Borden had remarried, his daughters Lizzie and Emma avoided their stepmother Abby, whom they believed had married their father for his money, and their late mother's brother John Morse was visiting to discuss some property issues on the fateful day of 4 August 1892. That was the day Andrew and Abby Borden were murdered with a hatchet.

Lizzie was tried and acquitted of their murders and officially the mystery of their deaths has never been solved. The house at 230 2nd Street is now a bed and breakfast with its supposedly haunted rooms themed around the unsolved case - its most-requested room is the guest room where Abby Borden was killed. Accommodation and tours are available, including day tours and night-time ghost tours.

Charles Island
MILFORD, CONNECTICUT
UTC-5

Charles Island has not one, not two, but three curses placed upon it. The first by a Paugussett chief, the second by notorious pirate Captain Kidd in order to keep his treasure safe, and the third is thanks to the 16th century Mexican Emperor Guatimozin, whose jinxed Aztec treasures are said to have been buried upon the tiny island.

Chestnut Hill Cemetery
EXETER, RHODE ISLAND
UTC-5

This small unassuming 10-acre cemetary opened in 1838 and holds a mere 1000 interments. But what Chestnut Hill lacks in grandeur it makes up for with its terrifying tales of vampires.

In the late 1800s, with little public understanding of disease, many people turned to folklore when tuberculosis wiped out entire families, leading to the New England Vampire Panic. The Browns were one such family decimated by TB. After losing his wife and two daughters and his son Edwin becoming ill, patriarch George decided that something must be done to save Edwin from the "vampire's grasp". So he decided to dig up the bodies of his deceased family members.

When he opened their graves, his wife and eldest daughter's bodies were heavily decomposed, but his daughter Mercy was remarkably intact - a sure sign of her vampirism. According to New England belief, finding blood in the heart of the dead revealed them as a vampire and the only way to remove the curse was to cast their heart into a fire. Mercy's heart and liver were burned, the ashes retrieved and mixed into a drink to help the ailing Edwin, but to no avail. He died two months later.

Ghost to Ghost Road Trip

Time zone **UTC-5**

John Zaffis Paranormal Museum
STRATFORD, CONNECTICUT

Paranormal researcher John Zaffis, nephew of celebrity ghosthunters Ed and Lorraine Warren, opened his museum in 2004 after receiving numerous objects from people claiming that their item was possessed by a spirit. In similar fashion to the Warrens' Occult Museum (which is now permanently closed) the items have been acquired from all over the world, each with a sinister story to tell – and often a malevolent spirit attached! But don't fret, everything has been ritually bound before being displayed. If you have an item you want to donate, the museum is happy to perform a ritual on it, just get in touch. The museum is currently searching for a new premises, but it'll be back soon, presumably bigger and better than ever!

> ❝ Don't fret, everything has been ritually bound before being displayed

TIP
WHY NOT CHECK OUT JOHN ZAFFIS' EXTENSIVE PARANORMAL TV CREDITS WHILE YOU'RE WAITING FOR THE MUSEUM TO REOPEN?

13

The Amityville House
LONG ISLAND, NEW YORK

Time zone **UTC-5**

In 1977 a sensational book captured the world's attention. *The Amityville Horror* by Jay Anson would go on to inspire a series of books and films about what happened at 112 Ocean Avenue in New York's Long Island suburb of Amityville, both on the notorious night of 13 November 1974 and thereafter. The tale has been mired in legal wrangling and controversy ever since. It's worth noting that the house, once known as High Hopes, has had its address changed, and been renovated completely to alter or remove the iconic windows and other features familiar from book covers and movies. Its current owners and neighbourhood residents alike are very unhappy with its notoriety and tend to refuse requests to discuss the location or its alleged events. This is not a house you can, or should, ever turn up to for a visit.

The reason that the house turned this quiet Long Island suburb into a paranormal media circus starts with the mass murder of his entire family - both parents, two brothers, and two sisters - by Ronald DeFeo Jr in 1974. DeFeo was a hard drug user and had a volatile relationship with his family. He was convicted of shooting all six of them in their beds. Up until his own death in prison in 2021 (aged 69), DeFeo gave interviews and filed lawsuits alleging that other members of the family, friends, and even the Mafia were responsible for the killings.

A year after the murders, the Lutz family bought and moved into the house, which still contained much of the DeFeo family's furniture, and it's here where the story really begins. Anson's book recounts that a friend of the Lutzes, concerned by the account of the murders, advised them to have the house blessed. It goes on to state that a local Catholic priest (whose name is changed in the book to protect his privacy) arrived to perform a blessing, but claimed he heard spectral voices telling him to "get out". Then the so-called Amityville horror really began. The Lutz family fled the property after 28 days, having been subjected to what the book claims were paranormal phenomena including ectoplasm, cloven hoofprints, poltergeist activity and much more.

Subsequent contractors, buyers and residents have reported no paranormal activity at the house.

DID YOU KNOW?!
THE FIRST THREE AMITYVILLE MOVIES WERE ACTUALLY SHOT AT A HOUSE IN TOMS RIVER, NEW JERSEY, WHICH WAS CONVERTED TO LOOK LIKE THE ICONIC PROPERTY AFTER AMITYVILLE AUTHORITIES REFUSED TO ISSUE FILM PERMITS.

Union Cemetery
EASTON, CONNECTICUT
UTC-5

Founded in the early 1700s, Union Cemetery is a beautiful, historical burial ground, and is said to be home to countless ghosts and ghouls. This infamous site was once deemed 'evil' and 'demonic' by famous paranormal investigators and self-styled demonologists, Ed and Lorraine Warren. With over 350 years of history in its grounds, it's little surprise that stories of hauntings have taken hold.

The majority of haunting reports from the cemetery relate to the 'White Lady'. A lonely female spirit in a white gown, she is said to wander around the cemetery and onto the nearby road. She has caused motorists to swerve or crash their vehicles, believing that they'd hit a pedestrian, only for the lady to have completely disappeared when they left their car. Other paranormal reports vary, but some of the most chilling are from a spirit, or demon, called "Red Eyes". Several visitors have reported a sensation of being watched, or feeling a stranger's hot breath against their neck. When they turn around, they're met with a pair of horrible, glowing red eyes, staring back at them from a distance.

Ghost to Ghost Road Trip

The Pine Barrens
NEW JERSEY
UTC-5

This enormous stretch of woodland has several stories hidden within its dense evergreens. There are the ghost towns, former colonial settlements now relics of a bygone era, left to disintegrate once coal was found in Pennsylvania. But the most famous Pinelands legend is the Jersey Devil. This cloven-hoofed, bat-winged creature with devilish horns, a forked tail and clawed hands was apparently spawned by a human woman. Mother Leeds gave birth to a seemingly normal 13th child, but it morphed into a goat-headed creature, let out a hideous scream and escaped up the chimney into the pines. Many suspected that Mother Leeds was a witch, and the child's father? Satan himself. Just like Bigfoot, many believers in the Jersey Devil propose that rather than a devil borne by a witch, he is simply an undiscovered species of animal who has long made the vast, remote wilderness his home.

The Jersey Devil has a few pals though: there are whispers that pirate Captain Kidd buried treasure on these Atlantic shores and still haunts the nearby beach, often seen with the Devil. A golden haired girl has also been spotted with the infamous cryptid. Rumour has it that she fell in love with the Jersey Devil's son, but her father wouldn't allow the union, prompting her to commit suicide. Other ghosts in the Pinelands include the Black Doctor, an African-American healer, who was supposedly banned from practising medicine on account of his race. Forced into seclusion in the Pine Barrens, he studied textbooks and Native remedies and uses his knowledge to help all those he comes across.

The Billop House
STATEN ISLAND, NEW YORK
UTC-5

Known variously as the Conference House and the Bentley Manor, this Staten Island residence was home to several generations of the Billopp family. In the late 18th century, Christopher Billopp was secretly a colonel in the British loyalist forces during the American Revolution. He allowed his home to be used to tend to injured British soldiers. Those that died were buried swiftly in unmarked graves. One evening, thinking that a servant girl was an American spy, Billop threw her down the stairs; her body met the same fate as the deceased redcoats. Today, it's thought that both she and innumerable British soldiers haunt the house. Now a museum, visits and tours are available during the museum's open season at limited times during weekends – although it should be noted that it focuses on its American Revolution history, not its paranormal associations.

The Paranormal Museum
ASBURY PARK, NEW JERSEY
UTC-5

A short walk from Asbury Park, seemingly hidden inside the Paranormal Books & Curiosities store, this museum offers tours as well as exhibits. It was founded in 2008 by Kathy Kelly, a lover of all things unexplained, to share her passion for folklore and local lore. The highlight is a skull supposedly of the Jersey Devil, a biped wyvern-like creature with the hooves, head of a horse or goat with horns and large leathery wings. Visits must be booked in advance but you receive a 60-minute guided tour with hands-on experiences with items in the collection.

Eastern State Penitentiary
PHILADELPHIA, PENNSYLVANIA
UTC-5

Opened in 1829, Eastern State Penitentiary aimed to revolutionise prisons with its Quaker-inspired system. Prisoners were meant to spend most of their solitary days reflecting and rehabilitating but, in reality, this deteriorated into psychological torture. Talking and letters from home were banned, and the only light they saw came from an "Eye of God" skylight.

Eventually, this mental torture became physical. A cast-iron gag over inmates' tongues, chained to their wrist shackles, stopped them speaking and, in at least one case, caused the inmate to bleed out after it ripped up his tongue. The Mad Chair, following the theory that mental illness spread via the body's circulation, mercilessly strapped prisoners in for days. This brutality ended in failure, and the notorious prison finally closed for good in 1971. Today, Eastern State Penitentiary embraces its grisly legacy with one of the US's top-rated haunted attractions, Halloween Nights. TV crews have captured disembodied voices and roaming apparitions. Guests themselves report a man in a crumbling, inaccessible guard tower and the "Soap Lady", who sits in the last cell in the women's cellblock, dressed in white. There's also cackling in cellblock 12, shadowy figures flitting along the walls in cellblock 6, and, in cellblock 4, a parade of ghostly faces.

These eerie stories have been corroborated since the 1940s and not even Al Capone, the most infamous inmate, was immune. Despite his cell having luxury rugs, oil paintings, and a radio, he was reportedly terrorised by a ghost named Jimmy.

> ❝ TV crews have captured roaming apparitions

Gettysburg Battlefield
GETTYSBURG, PENNSYLVANIA
UTC-5

This is a tremendously haunted town for one reason: the 1863 Battle of Gettysburg. With 50,000 casualties, it was by far the Civil War's bloodiest. No wonder the dead can't leave. In many locations such as Little Round Top, ghostly soldiers march in formation. On Culp's Hill, cries for help beg from the former burial pits, and on the Sachs Covered Bridge, mists rise from the water in the shape of men, and a ghost named "Henry" puffs on lit cigarettes. The Devil's Den is the most haunted of all. For centuries, the rocky outcrop was a Native American battleground, and early settlers reported phantom warriors. During the Battle of Gettysburg the Den became known as the "Slaughter Pen". A Texan soldier has been spotted since the 1970s, unkempt and shoeless, and a ghost rider appears to shouting and gunfire before instantly disappearing. The battlefield is now part of National Military Park. You can visit for free, but the guides are worth every penny.

Fort Delaware
PEA PATCH ISLAND, DELAWARE
UTC-5

On Pea Patch Island in the Delaware River sits Fort Delaware, built in the mid-1800s. During the Civil War, it housed Confederate captives (up to 12,595 at once). The fort was commanded by a man nicknamed General Terror, and its dark history of starvation, sickness, and overcrowding (plus prisoners fighting over rats to eat) caused dozens of deaths a day. Expect anything from a portrait turning into a skull to being prodded by poltergeists, from echoes of Civil War cannons to spirits peering at you around corners. Five-hour ghost tours are held in October, and it looks like you're in for a treat.

Ghost to Ghost Road Trip

Lake Shawnee Amusement Park
PRINCETON, WEST VIRGINIA
UTC-5

Closed since 1988, six deaths on the premises gave the park a reputation of being cursed. The land was also the site of the Lake Shawnee massacre, where three children died. Paranormal investigators claim to have heard children laughing while the swings move on their own in the empty park.

Westminster Burying Ground
BALTIMORE, MARYLAND
UTC-5

Established in 1786, the Westminster Burying Ground is one of the oldest places on our list. Attached to a church, it contains a veritable 'who's who' of Baltimore history. There are countless heroes of the 1812 and Revolutionary War buried within Westminster, including General Sam Smith, James McHenry and James Buchanan. However, it seems to be the more mysterious burials that excite visitors.

Following writer Edgar Allan Poe's sudden death in 1849, his burial couldn't be a simple affair. He was originally buried in an unmarked grave at the back of the grounds, and remained so for decades until, in 1875, local schoolchildren raised money for a memorial through a fundraising effort called "Pennies for Poe". The children were hugely successful in their project and a memorial to the late poet was built at the entrance of the grounds. His body was disinterred and re-buried beside his wife Virginia and his mother-in-law, Maria. Despite having a grand memorial, many locals believe that Poe is still restlessly wandering the graveyard, unsettled for eternity.

The Burying Ground is also home to the terrifying Screaming Skull of Cambridge. Reportedly the skull of an unknown murdered minister, it is said to be encased in cement with its jaw bound shut in an attempt to stifle its blood-curdling screams. According to legend, the skull would scream relentlessly and sounded so horrific in nature, that the sounds would torment the minds of those who heard them, sending them into madness.

TIP VISIT THE MOTHMAN MUSEUM, WHICH IS OPEN SEVEN DAYS A WEEK.

Point Pleasant
WEST VIRGINIA
UTC-5

Curses, winged creatures with hypnotic eyes and mysterious visits from men in black: Point Pleasant's history is anything but pleasant! Things didn't get off to a great start for this unassuming riverside town when, in 1774, beloved Shawnee warrior Cornstalk, his son and two other tribe members were executed by Revolutionary War fighters while carrying out a peace offering. Cornstalk is said to have cursed the town and it has suffered floods, fires, plane crashes, bridge collapses and more ever since. And there's more… In the 1960s, the town saw a spate of weird sightings of the Mothman, a creature with wings who terrorised rooftops, cars and pedestrians. Add in reports of visits from federal agents to 'hush' witnesses and one thing's for sure, the Mothman Museum and yearly Mothman Festival is a feast for fans of the freaky!

Trans-Allegheny Lunatic Asylum
WESTON, WEST VIRGINIA
UTC-5

Trans-Allegheny Lunatic Asylum is a lesson in how not to treat mental health issues. Overcrowding, poor sanitation, and limited light, heat, and furniture, combined with bloodletting, insulin coma therapy, and "ice-pick" transorbital lobotomies, led the hospital to become a violent house of horrors. Uncontrollable patients were kept in cages, and some even committed murder against fellow inmates. By the early 1900s, ghost stories were running riot. In the Civil War Wing lurks Ruth, pushing male visitors against the wall. A man who was bludgeoned to death by fellow patients haunts the spots where he died. Nine-year-old Lily sits in a toy-filled room, waiting to play; toys and a music box move by themselves. With a black mass called the "Creeper" crawling along the walls and screams from the ECT room ricocheting down the halls, this isn't somewhere anyone should linger.

Kenyon College
GAMBIA, OHIO
UTC-5

Kenyon College has a reputation for being one of the most haunted colleges in the US, with students reporting supernatural sightings every year. The ghost of Stuart Pierson has been spotted wandering Old Kenyon Residence Hall, as well as the nearby disused railroad tracks. The freshman was reportedly blindfolded and left on the tracks during a Delta Kappa Epsilon fraternity initiation in 1905 and tragically hit by an unscheduled train. The ghosts of those who perished in a fire in 1949 also haunt Old Kenyon. Many have experienced a ghost fire alarm, sudden chills and the feeling of a presence. Caples Residence Hall is haunted by student Doug Shafer, who was discovered at the bottom of the elevator shaft in 1979 – not long after the building opened. Students have reported feeling someone sit or lie on their bed as they fall asleep. There's also 'The Greenhouse Ghost', a diver who broke his neck and drowned in the Shaffer Pool, now the Shaffer Dance Studio, and the 'Gates of Hell' – stone pillars that are an omen of doomed friendships. Professor of Humanities Tim Shutt gives ghost tours and the university shares its haunted history via social media.

Ohio State Reformatory
MANSFIELD, OHIO
UTC-5

Masquerading as a French castle while aiming to reform young male offenders, Ohio State Reformatory ran from 1896 to 1990, when it closed due to a class action lawsuit claiming inhumane conditions. The ghosts of these abused boys and, from the mid-20th century, hardened adult criminals in maximum security, move furniture, slam doors, and throw pebbles at visitors. A guard killed in solitary confinement ("the hole") in 1932 still does his rounds, jabbing guests with his nightstick, and figures of shadow and light can be glimpsed, particularly in the attic.

TIP
BOOK THE PARANORMAL TOUR AFTER DARK FOR A HAIR-RAISING EXPERIENCE!

Waverly Hills Sanatorium
LOUISVILLE, KENTUCKY
UTC-5

Although Waverly Hills opened in 1910 as the USA's most advanced tuberculosis sanatorium, tens of thousands of patients died there and its 1961 closure was a godsend for TB sufferers. Why? Because its treatments were nothing short of torture. Balloons were implanted in the patients' lungs and filled with air, ribs and chest muscles were removed so the lungs had more oxygen, and lobotomies extracted whole lung lobes. Many recipients ended up in the 600-foot body chute, where visitors today spot spirits and balls of light. Other apparitions in the sanatorium itself include a little girl in the solarium, a woman with bleeding wrists pleading for help, and a white-coated man entering the ruined kitchen to the scent of baking bread. The worst is Room 502, used for patients with mental health issues. Two nurses committed suicide there, in 1928 and 1932, and while the first suffered from depression, the second is thought to have been tormented by the supernatural. Today, visitors to 502 report themselves and others acting out of character in disturbing and malicious ways.

Ghost to Ghost Road Trip

Colonial Park & Bonaventure Cemetery
SAVANNAH, GEORGIA
UTC-5

Savannah is often cited as one of the USA's most haunted cities, and with such a reputation, it's no wonder that its cemeteries are bursting with spooks. Colonial Park Cemetery is the oldest burial ground in the city, accepting its first permanent resident in 1750. The cemetery has countless interesting and thought-provoking gravestones, including Revolutionary War soldiers, victims of the Yellow Fever epidemic and historical figures such as Button Gwinnett - a signatory to the Declaration of Independence.

Some visitors have reported hearing strange voices, shadow people and the ghost of infamous murderer Rene Rondolier. Reportedly, he was convicted of murder and hung from a tree inside the cemetery ground. People claim to have seen him still hanging or even walking between the graves. Meanwhile, Bonaventure Cemetery was established in 1846 and is one of the most beautiful cemeteries in the country, but it also has its fair share of spooky goings on! Reports of children's laughter, baby's cries and a snarling pack of wild dogs heard within the cemetery grounds. The grave of six-year-old Gracie Watson is particularly popular, with visitors often bringing her toys and coins, placing them beside a statue resembling the child. Some claim to have seen Gracie herself, wandering through the cemetery as though in life.

DID YOU KNOW?!
BONAVENTURE CEMETERY IS FEATURED IN THE 1994 NOVEL MIDNIGHT IN THE GARDEN OF GOOD AND EVIL BY JOHN BERENDT AND THE CLINT EASTWOOD DIRECTED MOVIE OF THE SAME NAME.

The Bell Witch Cave
ADAMS, TENNESSEE
UTC-5

The Bell Witch is perhaps America's most famous haunting. A spirit tormented the Bell family between 1817 and 1821. She was a chatty character, identifying herself as Kate Batts, a disgruntled former neighbour. Batts supposedly claimed culpability for the death of the family patriarch, John Bell, although evidence suggests death by arsenic poisoning. The cave is on the Bell family's original property, and in some legends, the Witch is said to have assisted a lost child to safety - showing a kindness at odds with her reputation. Some believe she still lives in the cave.

Blackwater River
BLACKWATER RIVER STATE PARK, FLORIDA
UTC-5

A young woman with long black hair accompanied by the stench of rotting flesh haunts this popular tubing spot. Watch out though, she'll drag you to a watery grave if you fail to break free of her clutches. If you do escape, you might bump into a blood-soaked woman in a long white gown who has been spotted around the oldest white Atlantic cedar tree in the park. The river may flow past, but the unquiet spirits remain firmly anchored in their watery haunts.

> "The Bell Witch was quite a chatty character, identifying herself as Kate Batts, a disgruntled former neighbour with a grudge against the family"

Manchac Swamp
PONCHATOULA, LOUISIANA
UTC-6

About half an hour northwest of New Orleans, this ancient wetland isn't only riddled with alligators – some say it's home to far more sinister creatures. The most famous legend of Manchac Swamp, aka the Swamp of Ghosts, is that of Julia Brown. This voodoo priestess lived at the edge of the mossy wilderness. She aided Frenier locals with charms and healing, and was often seen sitting on her front porch singing haunting ditties with her guitar. In 1915, the day of Brown's funeral, a hurricane swept through Frenier, decimating the town and its neighbours of Ruddock and Napton, leaving nothing but ruins. Many people perished, swallowed up by the swamp water. One of Julia's songs predicted the town's fate, with the lyrics: "One day I'm going to die and take the whole town with me". This led to rumours that Julia had cursed Frenier and caused the storm, but it was likely just another of her many premonitions. Whether or not Julia hexed the town or not, she is said to still haunt the swamp, along with other townsfolk who died that day. Today, all that's left of the Frenier mass grave is the makeshift Frenier Cemetery which can only be visited on a tour from the Cajun Pride swamp tour company.

But it's not just witches and ghosts that haunt Manchac. The swamp is home to a werewolf-type creature: The Rougarou or loup-garou of Cajun folklore. This terrifying monster with glowing red eyes and razor-sharp teeth preys on misbehaving children. Visitors have reported growling and howls coming from deep within the marsh.

Bachelor's Grove Cemetery
COOK COUNTY, ILLINOIS
UTC-5

Bachelor's Grove Cemetery officially opened in 1836, however its first burials were earlier when workers who died building the Illinois and Michigan Canal were interred there. The cemetery is tiny, holding around 200 graves, and closed towards the end of the 20th century, but it has gathered quite the scary reputation.

After the cemetery closed to new burials, it was left to become overgrown. The image of a spooky overgrown cemetery was irresistible to some, and vandals, partying teenagers and grave-robbers gradually moved in. By the 1970s, unwelcome visitors were rife, and many of the remaining headstones were permanently destroyed. However, it wasn't the vandals that fired up a local media storm, but visitors with darker intent. Bachelor's Grove had become a hotbed for occult rituals of the most brutal kind. Local press reported that satanic cults would frequently gather at the cemetery and sacrifice animals in acts of black magic. The remains of animals and discarded ritualistic objects were frequently found by police at Bachelor's Grove, adding to the site's dark infamy. Rumours that the cemetery was used as a place for dumping bodies by several Chicago-based crime families, including Al Capone's, were also aired. Many had family members moved to more salubrious cemeteries at this time.

Unsurprisingly, there are many reported hauntings at Bachelor's grove. From twinkling lights and discs to women in white and dogs with glowing eyes. Strangest of all, an entire ghost farmhouse has been seen appearing in the middle of the cemetery, as though a portal to the past, or perhaps another world, had opened up.

Myrtles Plantation
ST FRANCISVILLE, LOUISIANA
UTC-6

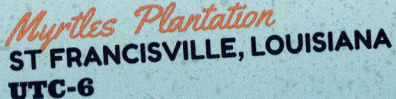

Once called the most haunted house in America, Myrtles Plantation is a paranormal triple threat. Allegedly built on a Native American burial ground, the site of at least one murder and a sinister poisoning, and a hub of African American plantation slavery to boot, it also boasts a spectral bloodstain that can apparently never be cleaned, a possessed mirror, and a voodoo-practising ghost. Leaning into its horrific haunted history, it offers accommodation, day and evening tours (both public and private), a coffee shop, and a restaurant specialising in Southern food.

Garnet
DRUMMOND, MONTANA
UTC-7

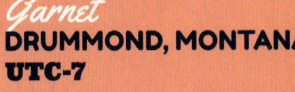

Garnet, a gold and garnet mining town, was established in 1895. It had a newspaper office, a drug store, hotels, and a school. By 1912, many of the mines had run dry and a fire destroyed half of the town. People moved back in the 1930s when gold prices increased, but WWII prompted residents to abandon the town in 1940. The Bureau of Land Management maintains the remaining buildings, making it Montana's best preserved ghost town. Many people believe Kelly's Saloon is haunted, with people hearing laughter and music when the town is empty in winter, and footsteps and doors closing inside the Wells Hotel raise questions.

Ghost to Ghost Road Trip

Lincoln Park Zoo
CHICAGO, ILLINOIS
UTC-5

Part of Lincoln Park Zoo sits upon land that was formally the final resting place of more than 30,000 people - 12,000 of whom likely still remain buried beneath the park today. The Chicago City Cemetery, open from 1843 to 1859, was located in the very spot many animals now call their homes and is likely responsible for the reported paranormal sightings of ghostly Victorian ladies, ominous flickering lights and doors slamming all by themselves in the Lion's House basement toilets.

The Cajun Sasquatch
HONEY ISLAND SWAMP, ST. TAMMANY PARISH, LOUISIANA
UTC-6

The Cajuns love a good cryptid, and just 40 miles away from New Orleans, in Honey Island Swamp, lurks a 500 pound sasquatch Cajuns call La Bête Noire (The Black Beast). This Louisiana Bigfoot was first seen in 1963 and captured on film by Harlan Ford, a retired air traffic controller who had taken up wildlife photography.

TIP
TAKE A HONEY ISLAND SWAMP TOUR BY BOAT – DON'T ATTEMPT TO EXPLORE ALONE. SWAMPS ARE DANGEROUS PLACES.

Villisca Ax Murder House
VILLISCA, IOWA
UTC-6

In June 1912 the little city of Villisca, Iowa, was rocked by a brutal axe murder incident. In the watches of the night between 9 and 10 June, six members of the Moore family - parents Josiah and Sarah, their children Herman Montgomery (11), Mary Katherine (10), Arthur Boyd (7), and Paul Vernon (5), and Mary Katherine's friends Ina Mae (8) and Lena Gertrude Stillinger (12), were all bludgeoned to death with an axe belonging to Josiah, which was found in the spare room where the visiting girls had been staying. No one has ever been convicted of the murders. An itinerant minister was tried twice and even confessed to the crime, but was acquitted due to mental illness. A number of paranormal investigations have been conducted, with photos, video and Electronic Voice Phenomena of its supposed haunting. Today the house at 508 E 2nd Street has been restored to its early 20th century condition, and functions as a museum.

Navajo Nation
NEW MEXICO
UTC-7

DID YOU KNOW?!
THE OFFICIAL LANGUAGE OF NAVAJO NATION IS DINÉ BIZAAD, MADE FAMOUS BY THE CODE TALKERS OF WORLD WAR II, WHO USED THEIR NATIVE LANGUAGE TO ENCRYPT US ARMY RADIO MESSAGES.

The Navajo Nation is the largest Native American reservation in the US, spanning northeastern Arizona, northwestern New Mexico and southeastern Utah and is home to the Navajo tribe who have occupied the area for hundreds of years. This area of desertland is policed by the Navajo Rangers, who take paranormal cases just as seriously as their regular investigations - which is just as well, as the landscape has experienced high levels of supernatural activity, from legendary monsters to ghosts and UFOS - although their federal training didn't quite prepare them for such an array of unearthly phenomena. Sightings of UFOs - often in the form of strange orbs of light - are common on the reservation. Coins often fall from the sky in the most haunted locations and Bigfoot has even been spotted wandering the ranges. But the most fearsome of all the paranormal encounters are the reports of Skinwalkers - shape-shifting evil witches who, according to the nation's retired rangers, no doubt exist. What's more, the rangers theorise that the supernatural activity is all linked, and related to the Navajo origin story. Navajo Nation is private, Federal Indian Land, and you must acquire a permit issued by the Navajo Parks and Recreation Department to visit. On top of this, make sure you treat the landscape and Navajo beliefs with utmost respect.

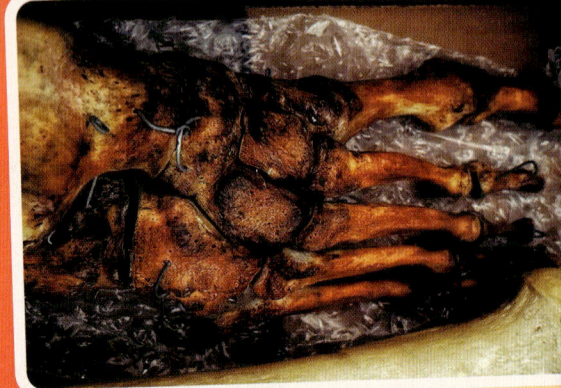

The Museum of Shadows
OMAHA, NEBRASKA
UTC-5

Located in the old market district of Omaha is the Museum of Shadows, housing all things macabre and paranormal. Owners Nate and Kaliegh Ratherman regularly receive new additions which are investigated before being included to the collection. Today they claim to have the largest collection of verified haunted objects in the world. Because of this it has been featured on numerous TV channels such as Discovery and the Travel Channel. The museum hosts many after-hours ghost hunts around its premises, inviting guests to bring their own paranormal equipment (or you can rent it from staff).

Flathead Lake
MONTANA
UTC-7

The Flathead Lake Monster is a gigantic horned serpent who locals have dubbed Flessie. It's been spotted since the 19th century, but the Kutenai tribe spoke of its existence through legends many years before. Witnesses report a terrifying 30-foot long eel-shaped creature with dark skin and greyish black eyes, while others suggest it looks more like a sturgeon.

Ghost to Ghost Road Trip

Hotel Monte Vista
FLAGSTAFF, ARIZONA
UTC-7

Dying to hear about the paranormal activity at Flagstaff's Hotel Monte Vista? Just ask the staff - each housekeeper, porter, cook and waiter has a story to tell. There's the one about the dancing couple in the cocktail lounge, locked in a ghostly embrace as they whirl around the floor. Or the baby in the basement, which torments passersby with its elusive cries.

The best apparition the Monte Vista plays host to can be found in the bar (where all good stories begin). In 1970, a trio of criminals robbed a nearby bank. They evaded capture, but one was shot while they escaped. Despite one of their number being wounded, the gang stopped in the Monte Vista's bar to celebrate - where, unfortunately, the man with the gunshot wound bled to death.

That hasn't stopped him from being cheerful in the afterlife. Both customers and staff have reported being startled by jolly, disembodied chants of "Good morning!" while barstools and drinks have been known to move on their own. Is it just coincidence... or evidence of a ghoulish crime caper?

The Bird Cage Theatre
TOMBSTONE, ARIZONA
UTC-7

The Bird Cage Theatre opened in 1881 and closed in 1892 with the closure of the town's silver mines. It had a bawdy reputation, hosting comedians, a strong woman act, magic shows, Cornish wrestling, and sex workers. Legendary lawman Wyatt Earp was a regular here and reputedly had an affair with a performer in one of the private rooms.

It's no surprise the Bird Cage Theatre is haunted - 26 people died here during shootouts and stabbings, or by suicide. One murder victim, a madam named Margarita, had her heart prised out of her chest with a stiletto dagger by a rival madam. Some visitors say they've seen a young woman wearing nothing but bloomers in the building - is it Margarita?

Tourists hear laughter and a piano being played inside the empty building, and some smell cigars and whiskey. Items move around the theatre of their own accord, and in the 1980s, invisible hands partially strangled the owner during a seance.

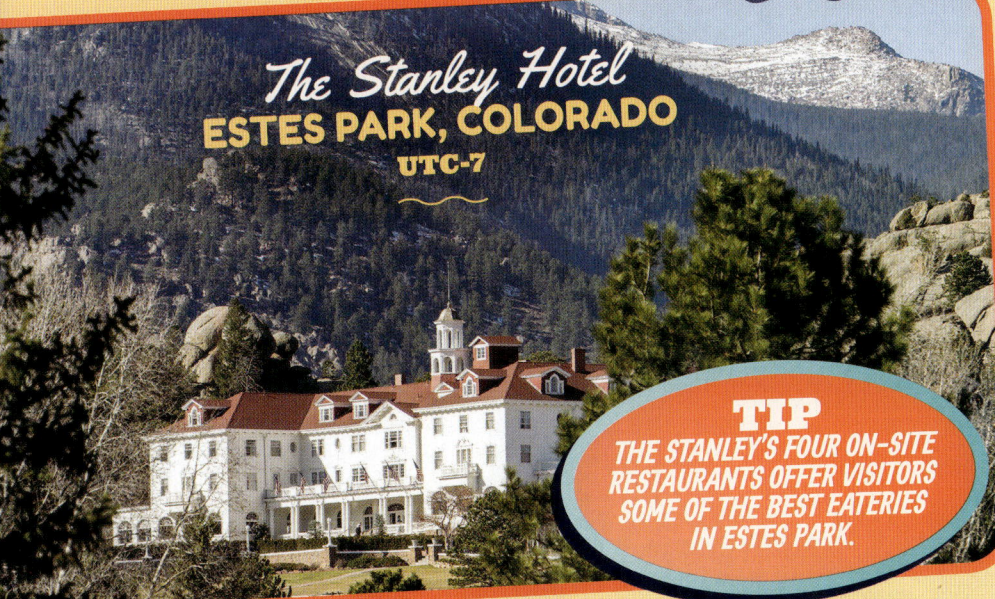

The Stanley Hotel
ESTES PARK, COLORADO
UTC-7

TIP
THE STANLEY'S FOUR ON-SITE RESTAURANTS OFFER VISITORS SOME OF THE BEST EATERIES IN ESTES PARK.

Roswell
NEW MEXICO
UTC-7

Ever happened upon a secret and then failed miserably to keep it? That pretty much sums up what happened at Roswell in the 1950s when a disc-shaped object (initially confirmed as a "flying saucer" before the story was retracted) appeared in a supposed alien crash near the town. Still, if the residents of the town at one point felt ill-treated by that web of (some say) lies, they've certainly made the most of the mysterious situation since. Roswell is packed with alien-related tourism that ranges from the serious to the outright silly. From the International UFO Museum, to the flying-saucer shaped Alien Caffeine Espresso Bar and fast-food chain, Roswell may be the UFOlogy tourism capital of the world.

Want to guarantee yourself a poor night's sleep? Book a night in The Stanley - an inspiration for Stephen King's *The Shining*, touted as the state's most haunted hotel. It seems strange that this dreamy 1909-built Rockies resort might actually be a nightmare, but if you feel the cool touch of a transparent hand, or hear the soft moans of troubled spirits, you'll probably want to get packing, stat.

There's barely a spot in The Stanley that isn't said to be haunted. Stephen King stayed in room 217, where the ghost of a chambermaid tidies guests' belongings while they sleep. In 428, there's a cowboy, and in 401, there's a malicious male ghost. Other ghosts are said to wander the property, including the hotel's founder, Freelan Oscar Stanley, who died of tuberculosis shortly after opening his business. Oh, and did we mention the on-site pet cemetery, where some of the beloved dogs and cats of days gone by slink about their afterlives?

Thankfully, The Stanley isn't afraid of its haunted reputation. The hotel hosts regular seances, and offers not one, but two ghost tours: one of them is even themed around *The Shining*.

Area 51 & the UFO Highway
NORTH OF LAS VEGAS, NEVADA
UTC-8

What does the US government keep at Area 51 that they don't want us Earthlings to discover? It's a mystery that's intrigued many a UFOlogist for years. This desert spot (seems like aliens apparently love these dusty locales) is more than just another military base; it's a codeword for secrecy and intrigue. Many believe that the relics from the Roswell "extraterrestrial crash site" (alongside, it's claimed, non-human corpses found in the area) were transplanted here. Unless you have high-level security clearance, there's little chance most of us will find out (and tourists are warned from entering, in all seriousness, in the strongest terms - it's closely guarded by armed personnel). On the upside, the less discreetly-named Extraterrestrial Highway running past the area, on the road north from Las Vegas, boasts fun attractions like the Little A'Le'Inn (pronounced Little Alien), the Alien Research Centre (museum and gift shop) and even the E.T. Fresh Jerky shop.

Shanghai Tunnels
PORTLAND, OREGON
UTC-8

The Shanghai Tunnels connected waterfront saloons, hotels, opium dens, gambling parlours, and more to the Willamette River's docks via trapdoors. From the mid-1800s to the early 1940s, they transported goods and, allegedly, thousands of kidnap victims a year. Women were sold as prostitutes and men as slaves to ship captains who needed crews. Rumour has it that the tunnels' existence was covered up to protect Portland's reputation, which is no surprise - once they fell in, many trafficked souls never got out, beaten, starved, and left for dead in holding cells. Visitors have experienced childlike whistling, fingers stroking them, attempts to knock them over, and even the ghost of "Sam", who turns off the lights and moves things around - he's friendly, though, so don't worry! Today, the only way to visit is on the Haunted Shanghai Tunnel Tour from Old Town Pizza and Brewing, where you'll hear about Nina, who died in the late 1800s and can be seen watching diners in a black dress or wandering the basement, snatches of her perfume caught on the air.

Bodie
MONO COUNTY, CALIFORNIA
UTC-8

Bodie, a former gold mining town in the Eastern Sierra Nevada Mountains, is California's most famous ghost town. Founded in 1859, it was a bustling town by 1880, full of gunfights, gambling, and girls galore, with two churches compared to 65 saloons!

Its decline began in 1882, although people lived there until the 1940s. Bodie became a State Historic Park in 1962, and the town preserves buildings as they are; it doesn't restore them. This "state of arrested decay" adds to Bodie's eerie quality. The town still has 100 structures standing, including the Bodie Jail, where John Wayne was photographed. But beware the Bodie Curse! Taking anything from the town - even a stone - will curse you with bad luck until you return the item. Some people think that Bodie's ghosts stand guard over the town, and people claim to see and hear various spectres.

The Roosevelt
LOS ANGELES, CALIFORNIA
UTC-8

The Roosevelt is LA's longest-operating hotel. The towering landmark opened in 1927, at the height of America's gilded party age. Hollywood's high flyers breezed through its Spanish-style lobby, swam in its pretty pool, and stayed up all night in its 300 glamorous rooms. If you're a film fanatic, you're in luck: the ghosts of a few stars have been known to make a cameo.

Marilyn Monroe filmed her first commercial in the hotel swimming pool. As her career reached new heights, she frequented one of the hotel's pool cabanas, which was installed with a full-length mirror. Some time after the actress' death, a maid was cleaning the room, and a glum blonde bombshell appeared in the mirror. The maid whipped around, shocked, but there was nobody standing there...

And what about the muffled sound of the bugle, emanating from room 928? Apparently, that's the ghost of Academy Award nominee Montgomery Clift, who is still practising for his role as an army trumpeter in 1953's *From Here To Eternity*.

Ghost to Ghost Road Trip

Alcatraz Island
SAN FRANCISCO, CALIFORNIA
UTC-8

A favourite spot for dark tourism, Alcatraz was considered inescapable. During the Civil War, it housed military prisoners, and from 1934 to 1963 it served as a federal prison for incorrigible villains such as Al Capone and the original Machine Gun Kelly, a Tennessee gangster.

It's notoriously haunted. Centuries-old Native American history documents The White Rock being thronged by evil spirits, and tribal lawbreakers would be banished here to live among them. Today, visitors report crying, moaning, deafening clanging, and a malevolent feeling in cellblock C's laundry room, where hitman Abie Maldowitz ("Butcher") was killed in the 1940s by a fellow inmate.

The stories don't stop there. While Alcatraz was still operational, guards reported cannon fire and gunshots so real that they believed the prisoners were escaping. In the old hospital ward, screams echo from inmates who were secured to a table until they calmed down.

If this wasn't enough, in D block, the most haunted section, a man was found strangled in cell 14D in the 1940s. Rumour has it that the night before, he was screaming that a glowing-eyed monster known as "The Thing" was trying to kill him. Many visitors report being smothered in a horrific sense of cold, and the cell is often almost 20 degrees below the rest of the block.

TIP
CHECK OUT THE QUEEN MARY'S ONBOARD SHOPS FOR A RANGE OF NAUTICAL (AND HAUNTED) SOUVENIRS.

The Museum of Death
HOLLYWOOD, CALIFORNIA
UTC-8

What is creepier than an entire museum devoted to death? The Museum of Death is a morbid, disturbing gallery that's not for the faint of heart. Boasting a large collection of serial killer artwork, letters and items, it's a chilling delve into the darkside of death. Crime scene photographs, autopsy footage, mortuary equipment and even torture devices are all on display, along with the head of a French serial killer and a significant number of taxidermied animals. The original LA venue is temporarily closed, but the museum's founders, JD Healy and Cathee Shultz, have opened a second premises in New Orleans so you can get your macabre fix if you happen to be in The Big Easy.

RMS Queen Mary
LOS ANGELES, CALIFORNIA
UTC-8

On the day of her launch in 1934, English psychic Lady Mabel Fortescue-Harrison predicted this luxury transatlantic liner would "know her greatest fame and popularity when she never sails another mile". She was right – since becoming a land-based hotel, the RMS Queen Mary has become one of LA's quirkiest tourist attractions. Voted one of the most haunted places in America, a gaggle of ghosts occupy the ship. One fateful night in 1948, a third-class passenger staying in Stateroom B340 died in mysterious circumstances; guests have felt his presence at the end of their bed, even pulling off the covers as they sleep. There's also the 18-year-old crewman, crushed to death by a door in 1966, whose spirit whistles through the corridors.

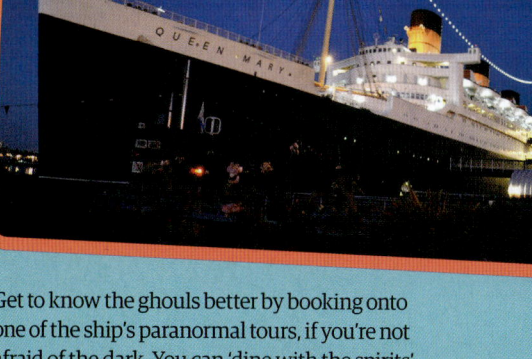

Get to know the ghouls better by booking onto one of the ship's paranormal tours, if you're not afraid of the dark. You can 'dine with the spirits'; an experience that includes a bite to eat in the award-winning Sir Winston's Restaurant, before exploring below deck on a haunted history tour. Or, if you dare, take part in a ghost hunt with a paranormal investigator, which visits places even the hotel guests are forbidden to go... ★

Location
Washington D.C.
~
Time zone
UTC-4

Weird WASHINGTON D.C.

The country's capital has a slew of iconic buildings but also some lesser-known stranger places

WORDS **Jack Griffiths**

Main The Washington Monument and the United States Capitol are two of the city's most famous buildings

Opposite right Two sphinxes sit either side of the entrance leading to a library, museum and even office space

Opposite bottom The catacombs aren't freely open to the public but guided tours are available

Washington D.C.

Washington, D.C. is awash with famous sights, many instantly recognisable the world over. The city differs from other US metropolises with its skyscraper-free skyline, thanks to 1910's Height of Buildings Act, allowing for better views of cultural structures such as the Washington Monument. D.C. was founded in 1790, chosen by George Washington, who lends his name to the city, to serve as the permanent capital of the USA, officially relocating the federal government to the city from its temporary home in Philadelphia in 1800. Washington, D.C. was selected due to its location in the middle of the northern and southern states and among two rivers. French engineer Pierre Charles L'Enfant was tasked with designing the all-new city, taking inspiration from his hometown of Paris and constructing it upon a grid system.

After a tumultuous period during the War of 1812 and the American Civil War, with the United States Capitol even set alight by British forces in the former, Washington, D.C. only grew in stature. Ever since the advent of the railways in the early 1800s, tourism has become big business with 24 million visitors to the National Mall and its iconic monuments alone, every year.

The hosts the country's oldest continuously-functioning fish market and is very international in its outlook, with 15 per cent of citizens speaking a language other than English. The buildings have a classical Greek and Roman architectural influence and incorporate ancient Egyptian and medieval European elements. One of D.C.'s most iconic structures is the Washington Monument, a 16.8 metre (55 feet) tall white granite and marble obelisk. Its cornerstone and many of its interior stones feature Freemason inscriptions, an organisation whose influence can be seen in many of the city's buildings. They even left their mark on the White House – until President Truman, a Freemason himself, ordered the removal of the masonic stones during the rebuilding of the property in 1949 and sent them to the Grand Lodge of the District of Columbia's Headquarters, who distributed one to each of the country's grand lodges.

Behind the formulaic facade of its federal district lies a whole lot of weird, from horror film locations to secret underground passageways, there is more to D.C. than meets the eye – it's even speculated that the city's very design is symbolic, harbouring a hidden occult meaning...

House of the Temple
DUPONT CIRCLE

The key Freemason temple stands a mile north from the White House and is a very impressive building in its own right. Young architect John Russell Pope was instructed to spare no expense in its construction and his design was inspired by one of the Seven Wonders of the Ancient World: the Mausoleum of Halicarnassus. The temple is the headquarters of the Scottish Rite of Freemasonry, Southern Jurisdiction, and was first opened in 1915 after taking four years to build.

Inside is a collection based on famous Scottish poet and Freemason Robert Burns as well as the city's first public library, which contains more than a quarter of a million works of Masonic literature. While Pope went on to design two other of Washington's most famous buildings, the National Archives building and the Jefferson Memorial, the House of the Temple became the resting place for a number of prominent Masons. More recently, the building featured in Dan Brown's *Lost Symbol*.

Catacombs
FRANCISCAN MONASTERY OF THE HOLY LAND IN AMERICA

When you think of catacombs, you probably think of Paris, perhaps even Rome, but not Washington, D.C.! However, D.C. has its very own version, under the city streets. This web of passages lies under beneath the Franciscan Monastery of the Holy Land but, unlike its European counterparts, it is nowhere near as ancient, or real. In fact, it was only opened in the early 20th century and only one of the graves is genuine. The monastery's monks concocted the catacombs to cater for people who couldn't afford to travel to their European equivalents and to further educate local monks. The sole authentic grave is of a child, believed to have been a martyr originally buried in Rome's Catacomb of St Callistus. The rest of the subterranean tunnels are filled with superficial tombs, altars and chapels.

> ❝ *The pentagram, a five-pointed star symbol used by the Masons, is formed by the city's streets*

Pentagrams of Washington, D.C.
THROUGHOUT CITY

Freemasonry plays a major part in Washington, D.C.'s heritage. George Washington wore a Masonic uniform when laying the cornerstone of the United States Capitol. Additionally, the foundations of the Smithsonian Institution Building and The National Cathedral were also laid after a Masonic ritual.

As a result, the pentagram, a five-pointed star symbol used by the Masons, is formed by the city's streets. This phenomenon was revisited with renewed attention after the release of Dan Brown's 2009 novel, *Lost Symbol*, the sequel to the best-selling, *The Da Vinci Code*. It's believed that geometric layout of the Dupont Circle, Logan Circle, Scott Circle, Washington Circle, Mount Vernon Square and the White House purposely form a pentagram. Additionally, the United States Capitol building (the seat of Congress), sits on the eastern edge of the National Mall, where all of Washington's main landmarks are. Freemasons place importance on the phrase 'Look to the East' as that is where both the sun rises and where the highest-ranking officer sits in their lodges.

There are other theories about the city's layout. The one with the most legs is that the White House, the Capitol and the Supreme Court were all built in a so-called Federal Triangle to represent the executive, legislative and judicial sections of government. Another hypothesis is that the White House, the Jefferson and Lincoln Memorials and the Capitol were all built in their exact places to form the masonic Square and Compasses symbol. Additionally, a number of the Circles all have six main streets leading into them, meaning the number of the beast, 666, is embedded into D.C.'s city plan.

Space Window
WASHINGTON NATIONAL CATHEDRAL

Stained glass windows are nothing new in places of worship but, what about one with a space rock in it? The Scientists and Technicians Window, to give it its full name, has sat proudly in the city's National Cathedral's nave since 1973. What sets it apart is the extra-terrestrial chunk of basalt rock at its centre.

It was created to honour the people at NASA that achieved the lunar landing. The three Apollo 11 astronauts, Neil Armstrong, Buzz Aldrin and Michael Collins, added a Moon rock to the display making it even more cosmic. The Space Window is one of the most visited areas of the cathedral, along with the cathedral's Darth Vader grotesque, but that's a story for a different time.

The Exorcist Steps
GEORGETOWN

Famous steps are a thing. You've got the Potemkin Stairs in Ukraine, the epic entrance to the city of Odessa and, in New York City, the Joker Stairs which were featured in the 2019 film of the same name (and again in its 2024 sequel). Washington has the Exorcist Steps.

The 75 steps are iconic for featuring in the 1973 horror flick, *The Exorcist*. The film, which was shot in surrounding Georgetown, is a classic of its genre and many fans travel to see them. First built in 1895 as a simple shortcut between Prospect Street and M Street, the filmmakers made a few temporary changes when they featured in the movie. The steps were padded to break the fall of the character Father Damien Karras and a false front added to one of the buildings to make it more tightly wrap around the steps. For some, this is just a public right of way but for many others the steps have an atmosphere to them, especially when they get covered in ivy and a chilly wind or fog draws in. ★

Above The Exorcist Steps were padded during the filming of the horror flick to cushion the stuntman's fall

Opposite top There is a lot of speculation around the origins of the National Mall and whether it is laid out to a hidden design

Opposite left A rock from the Moon is slotted into the window's centre, which luckily survived damage in a 2011 earthquake

DID YOU KNOW?!

SITUATED IN THE HISTORIC DISTRICT OF GEORGETOWN, THE EXORCIST STEPS WERE OFFICIALLY RECOGNISED AS A LANDMARK FOR THEIR ROLE IN CINEMATIC HISTORY AND COMMEMORATED WITH A PLAQUE JUST IN TIME FOR HALLOWEEN 2015.

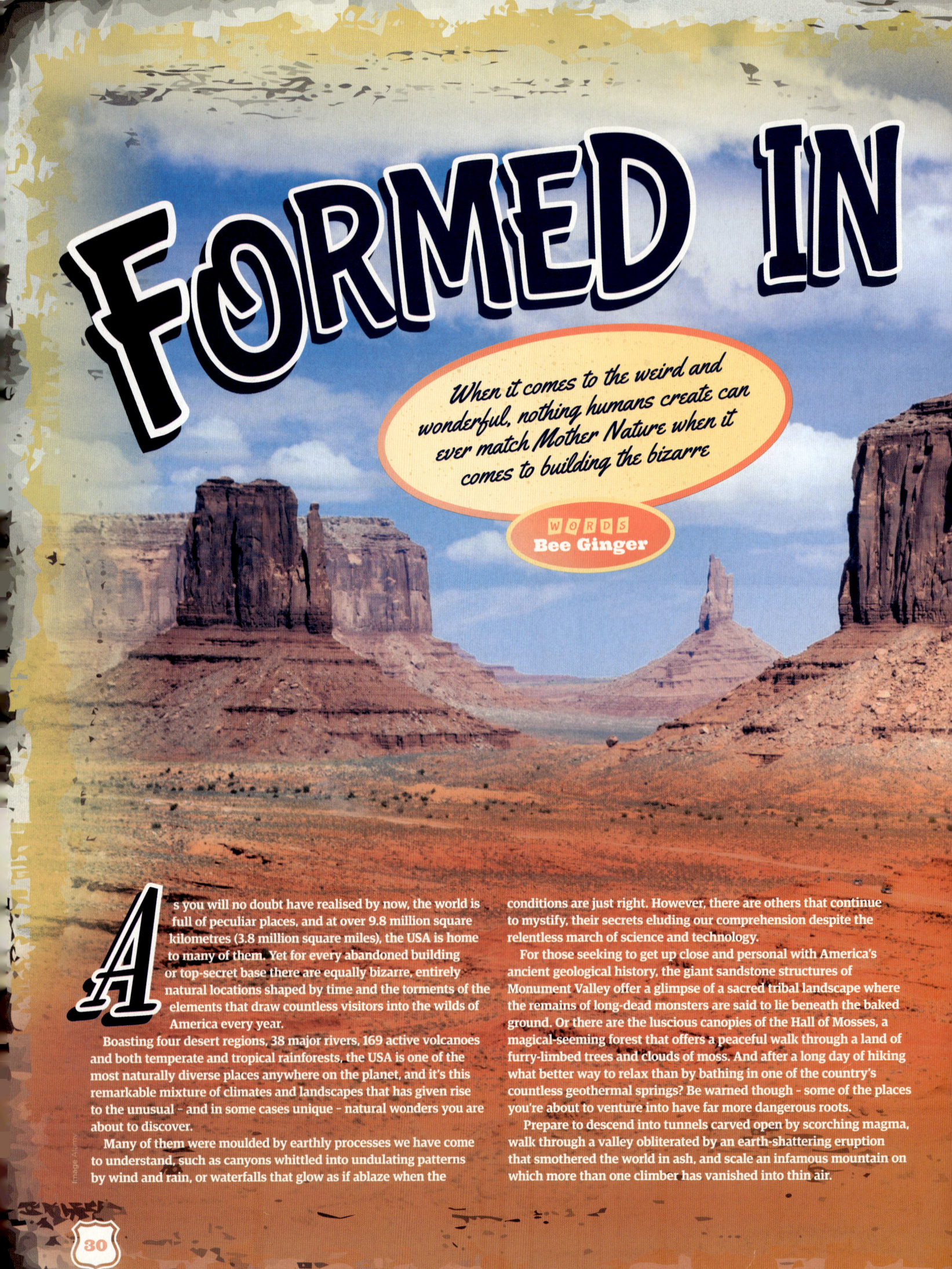

FORMED IN

When it comes to the weird and wonderful, nothing humans create can ever match Mother Nature when it comes to building the bizarre

WORDS
Bee Ginger

As you will no doubt have realised by now, the world is full of peculiar places, and at over 9.8 million square kilometres (3.8 million square miles), the USA is home to many of them. Yet for every abandoned building or top-secret base there are equally bizarre, entirely natural locations shaped by time and the torments of the elements that draw countless visitors into the wilds of America every year.

Boasting four desert regions, 38 major rivers, 169 active volcanoes and both temperate and tropical rainforests, the USA is one of the most naturally diverse places anywhere on the planet, and it's this remarkable mixture of climates and landscapes that has given rise to the unusual – and in some cases unique – natural wonders you are about to discover.

Many of them were moulded by earthly processes we have come to understand, such as canyons whittled into undulating patterns by wind and rain, or waterfalls that glow as if ablaze when the conditions are just right. However, there are others that continue to mystify, their secrets eluding our comprehension despite the relentless march of science and technology.

For those seeking to get up close and personal with America's ancient geological history, the giant sandstone structures of Monument Valley offer a glimpse of a sacred tribal landscape where the remains of long-dead monsters are said to lie beneath the baked ground. Or there are the luscious canopies of the Hall of Mosses, a magical-seeming forest that offers a peaceful walk through a land of furry-limbed trees and clouds of moss. And after a long day of hiking what better way to relax than by bathing in one of the country's countless geothermal springs? Be warned though – some of the places you're about to venture into have far more dangerous roots.

Prepare to descend into tunnels carved open by scorching magma, walk through a valley obliterated by an earth-shattering eruption that smothered the world in ash, and scale an infamous mountain on which more than one climber has vanished into thin air.

Natural Wonders

THE USA

The Navajo name for Monument Valley is Tsé Bii' Ndzisgaii, meaning 'Valley of the Rocks'

Fly Geyser
WASHOE COUNTY, NEVADA
UTC-8

In 1916, a team of diggers tasked with sourcing water in the sun-baked Black Rock Desert in northwest Nevada found their spades biting into unusually warm soil. They'd found water all right – and it was almost boiling. A natural geothermal pool lay exposed to the open air, but the crew soon realised that it was poorly suited to agriculture and swiftly moved on. In time a jagged cone of calcium formed, a column of red and white that would come to be known as the Wizard. It stood alone above the surrounding Hualapai Flat for 48 years until the same water source was disturbed again, this time by an energy company drilling in a nearby spot. On this occasion the water was deemed too cool, and the company attempted to seal the hole they'd dug. But Mother Nature had other ideas. Composed of mineral deposits, a multicoloured mound began to take shape, at the top of which a half-metre (two-foot) geyser continues to spray water up to 3.5 metres (12 feet). The Fly Geyser, which derives its incredible hues from thermophilic algae, is situated on private land, so visitors must book a walking tour prior to their arrival.

Valley of 10,000 Smokes
KATMAI NATIONAL PARK AND PRESERVE, ALASKA
UTC-4

Flat, barren and scarred by deep gorges, the Valley of 10,000 Smokes brings the surrounding trees of Katmai National Park to an abrupt halt, a wide stretch of compacted ash smothering virtually all life for miles. This 145-square-kilometre (56-square-mile) terrain was created when the Novarupta volcano erupted in June 1912. This immense explosion saw pyroclastic flows surging out across the surrounding area, which was soon blanketed beneath a sheet of ash and pumice up to 200 metres (650 feet) deep. The eruption, which caused the collapse of Mount Katmai over ten kilometres (six miles) away, cooled the northern hemisphere by one degree Celsius (two Fahrenheit).

The valley didn't receive its fitting name until Robert F Griggs explored the area and witnessed steam billowing out of the countless fumaroles that pockmark the valley while writing about the aftermath of the eruption for the National Geographic Society in 1916. While the blast didn't kill anybody due to the volcano's isolation, Griggs estimated that had a similar eruption occurred in Manhattan every living thing on the island would have been destroyed and the explosion heard in Chicago – almost 1,290 kilometres (800 miles) away. Today, visitors can walk along the valley floor on guided tours safe in the knowledge that the once formidable volcano that shaped it is now dormant.

Subway Cave
OLD STATION, CALIFORNIA
UTC-6

California is known as the Golden State due to the discovery of vast deposits of the precious metal beneath its soil in 1848, which triggered a gold rush. But gold isn't the only glowing substance hidden in the depths of America's wealthiest state. Approximately 24,000 years ago, a monumental volcanic eruption spewed tons of lava out of vents near Old Station, a former military outpost and coach stop in the north of California. The searing lava poured into fissures as it raced towards Hat Creek Valley. The molten liquid closer to the surface then began to cool, but the magma below it continued to burn, carving out a series of subterranean caves and tunnels, the largest of which is the Subway Cave. Spanning 7.5 metres (25 feet) wide and five metres (17 feet) high, this lava tube can easily accommodate an adult walking upright, and it draws visitors by the thousands from May to October every year. As well as the main tunnel, which is accessed via a staircase that descends into the earth, those coming to marvel at this natural feat of geological engineering will also encounter two sealed caves: the Sanctum and Lucifer's Cul-de-Sac.

Top left Including the mound upon which it stands, Fly Geyser measures 1.5 metres (five feet) tall

Above left The eruption lasted for around 60 hours and sent a 32-kilometre-high (20-mile) plume of ash and smoke up into the sky

Above Located in Lassen National Forest, the Subway Cave is 0.5 kilometres (0.3 miles) long

TIP
FOLLOW THE SELF-GUIDED SULPHUR SPRINGS TOUR ROUTE IN THE NATIONAL PARK SERVICE APP.

Natural Wonders

Left On average, Mount Shasta claims the life of one climber every year. In 1965, John Nezza vanished while scaling the mountain in a case with eerie similarities to Carl Landers

Bottom Visitors hoping to explore the springs should beware of potentially boiling water – and the rotten-egg smell!

Mount Shasta
SISKIYOU COUNTY, CALIFORNIA
UTC-8

Looming over the surrounding peaks of the Cascade Range, Mount Shasta is arguably America's most mysterious natural place. The highest of four overlapping volcanic cones (Hotlum, Shastina, Sargents Ridge and Misery Hill) and home to seven named glaciers, Shasta is rated as the fifth most dangerous volcano in the US. But the magma that bubbles below its surface isn't the only thing this 4,320-metre (14,170-foot) giant hides.

Local Native American tribes believe Shasta is home to powerful spirits, among them Skell, a mighty sky spirit who came back from the dead to defeat Llao, a spirit of the underworld. Others say the mountain is the site of a subterranean city built by a race called the Lemurians. After fleeing their sinking Pacific home, they bored tunnels beneath the mountain, from which these tall, pale figures occasionally emerge, clad in flowing robes, to wander the mountainside.

Other bizarre reports include strange voices and lights, UFOs, and Bigfoot and Batsquatch (a creature that has the appearance of a man with long, bat-like wings) sightings. While the merits of these claims are debatable, one unsettling tale continues to baffle even the most experienced climbers.

In May 1999, 69-year-old Carl Landers, a veteran climber, vanished while attempting to reach the summit alongside two friends. Having failed to do so on a previous expedition, Landers was determined to reach the top of the mountain, and despite complaining of feeling unwell to his companions while camped at around 2,700 metres (8,860 feet) he pressed on, encouraged by his friends to get an early start before they caught up with him later. They would never see Carl again.

Despite extensive searches at the time, which deployed canine rescue teams and helicopters equipped with infrared sensing devices, no trace of Landers or even his equipment has ever been found. Carl was last spotted in open ground well above the tree line, and there were no reports of any avalanches on the day of his disappearance. It's as though the mountain swallowed him whole.

Sulphur Springs
SULPHUR SPRINGS, NEW MEXICO
UTC-6

Littered with rusting cars and dilapidated wooden shacks, the area surrounding the Sulphur Springs of New Mexico's Jemez Mountains resembles an abandoned town from a horror film. However, this place was once home to a thriving health spa complete with bathhouses and a three-storey log cabin. Here guests would soak in the pungent waters of the geothermal pools to heal wounds, with some even daring to drink it in order to ease internal ailments. Operated by the family of businessman and politician Mariano Otero, who had previously mined the area for sulphur, the spa offered baths for as little as 50 cents - or for free if a visitor appeared to be destitute. Unfortunately, the cabin burned down in the 1970s, forcing the spa to close. Since then the acidic springs, mud pots and fumaroles have been left to hiss and bubble in relative peace, although in the 1980s Los Alamos National Laboratory did set up an experimental geothermal well as part of their efforts to study a volatile landscape boasting natural features that are rare in the western US.

Antelope Canyon
PAGE, ARIZONA
UTC-7

It's not difficult to see why this is the most-photographed slot canyon in the world. Actually two canyons – Upper and Lower – Antelope Canyon is a long, narrow and very deep gauge cut out of Navajo sandstone by wind and rain erosion. Measuring 200 metres (650 feet) and 400 metres (1,300 feet) in length respectively, the canyons, located in Lake Powell Navajo Tribal Park, are only accessible on guided tours. Upper Canyon is easier to navigate and offers higher peaks, and in the summer months shafts of light beam down through holes in the rock to create stunning displays ideal for photographers, who come in their droves to snap the ripples of stone. Despite Arizona's warm summer climate, the canyon is susceptible to flash flooding. In August 1997, 11 tourists were sadly drowned in Lower Canyon when a storm in the nearby city of Page sent a torrent of water rushing into the narrow passages.

The Wave
MARBLE CANYON, ARIZONA
UTC-7

Woven into undulating patterns as though by a god with an eye for optical illusions, the mesmerising shapes and colours of Arizona's Wave make for an otherworldly view of a time when dinosaurs roamed America. Situated over 1,585 metres (5,200 feet) above sea level in the Coyote Buttes, these swirling sandstone dunes were moulded by rain and slow winds over 190 million years ago, causing them to calcify both vertically and horizontally. Yet while they hardened long ago, these slopes can still be damaged. In order to preserve them, restrictions are in place to limit the number of visitors a day, and they must have a permit to explore the ravine. Permits are given out via a lottery scheme, which involves a $9 (approximately £7) fee.

Monument Valley
COLORADO PLATEAU, ARIZONA-UTAH BORDER
UTC-6

Looming over the arid Colorado Plateau, the sandstone towers of this ancient basin reveal a fascinating part of America's distant past. Forced upwards by tectonic shifts that began 300 million years ago, the buttes were shaped by a mixture of water and wind erosion. Reaching skyward to heights of up to 300 metres (1,000 feet) above the valley floor (which is coloured a deep red due to the presence of iron oxide in the siltstone), the buttes vary significantly in size and shape, but all of them are stratified into three main layers of rock.

Straddling the Utah-Arizona border, the valley is a Tribal Park considered sacred by the Navajo people. According to legend, the rocky spires of the Three Sisters formation are in fact the remains of vanquished monsters who were turned to stone by divine beings known as the Twins.

Among many other stunning formations are the Totem Pole, Rooster Rock and King-on-his-Thone, which really does look like a ruler surveying his kingdom from a colossal stone chair.

Visitors to the valley are required to pay a fee before driving through it on a 27-kilometre (17-mile) track, but there are some spots, such as Mystery Valley, that can only be reached with the help of a guide from a designated Navajo tour company. The main loop tour takes around two and a half hours. For those seeking a true Wild West experience, there is the option to saddle up and explore the area on horseback.

Left The Navajo name for the upper canyon is Tsé bighánílíní ('the place where water runs through the rocks')

Left middle The footprints of dinosaurs have been unearthed in Coyote Buttes, including imprints made by grallators, bipedal theropods who stood around 75 centimeres (30 inches) tall

Left below At 1,892 metres (6,207 feet), Merrick Butte is the tallest formation in the valley

Top right Once the scene of a bustling mining industry, Bonnie Claire was gradually abandoned in the early 1950s

Below It may look static, but Slumgullion is actually a torrent of flowing earth, a landslide in slow motion

Sailing Stones
BONNIE CLAIRE, NYE COUNTY, NEVADA
UTC-4

Stones are many things, but mobile isn't usually one of them. That is unless the stone in question is lying in the dry lakebed of Bonnie Clare Playa in central Nevada. Found on the fringes of a closed valley known as the Sarcobatus Flat not far from the abandoned mining town after which it was named, the lakebed can, in the right conditions, be covered in a layer of ice in the winter. When it fractures it breaks up into sheets, which are then taken up by the wind and moved over the ground, in turn pushing stones across the cracked soil. Well, that's the scientific explanation anyway, but given there's a ghost town a stone's throw away, perhaps there's something else that causes them to move…

> "There's a ghost town a stone's throw away"

DID YOU KNOW?!
IN 1873 A MAN CALLED ALFRED GRINER PACKER JOINED A GROUP ATTEMPTING TO TRAVEL PAST SLUMGULLION THROUGH THE SAN JUAN MOUNTAINS. HE WAS LATER DISCOVERED TO HAVE KILLED AND EATEN HIS FIVE COMPANIONS.

Slumgullion
LAKE CITY, COLORADO
UTC-7

It might look as though it's simply part of the mountainous landscape of Hinsdale County, Colorado, but this mass of earth is actually moving. When you think of a landslide, a torrent of mud and rocks probably comes to mind, but some landslides take their time. Tilting the trees as it goes, Slumgullion has been shifting down Lake Fork Valley since a section of the Lake City calderon (a large hollow left behind after a volcanic eruption) broke free from a mountain named Mesa Seco over 700 years ago. This collapse dammed a fork of the Gunnison River, in turn birthing Lake San Cristobel. 400 years later, a second slide began, which continues to inch its way down the valley at a rate of seven metres (23 feet) per year in a prime example of a process known as mass wasting, whereby gravity forces a section of earth or rock down a slope. Today it is six kilometres (four miles) long and encompasses over a thousand acres of land.

Hanging Lake
GLENWOOD SPRINGS, COLORADO
UTC-7

Said to have been stumbled upon by a gold prospector, Colorado's Hanging Lake is a treasure worth the hike. Fed by mountain springs, as well as the waters of Dead Horse Creek and possibly also an underground source, this stunning turquoise pool is ringed by travertine and derives its beautiful colours from carbonate minerals. Despite its tranquil appearance, the lake, which pools at an elevation of 2,323 metres (7,323 feet), was made in rather dramatic fashion when over an acre of the valley floor gave way along a fault line. Anyone steadfast enough to hike the trail up to the lake will be greeted with breathtaking views, but it's worth noting that at such altitudes the air can become very thin.

TIP HIKERS TO HANGING LAKE ARE REQUESTED TO GREET EACH OTHER ON THE TRAIL.

Above Whether you're hiking or biking to Hanging Lake, a permit is required for all visitors

Below Visitors are advised to park their vehicles at the base of the dome to avoid the risk of driving straight into the punchbowl

Diana's Punchbowl
ROUND MOUNTAIN, NEVADA

Time zone **UTC-8**

Also known as the Devil's Cauldron, this geothermal pool is approximately 15 metres (50 feet) across and nine metres (30 feet) deep. Accessed by a single track running through Monitor Valley, its water can reach temperatures of 93 degrees Celsius (200 Fahrenheit) and is estimated to be over 30 metres (100 feet) deep. One of over 300 hot springs in Nevada (more than any other state), this yawning hole should be approached with caution. One Native American legend tells of a young couple who came to the pool to try to retrieve some eagle eggs from the nests that line the lip of this depression, which is set within a travertine (a fragile type of limestone) dome. In order to reach the eggs, the man gripped the woman by the ankles and lowered her down. Sadly, she slipped from his grasp and plunged into the water. Her lover dived in to save her, but the pair tragically drowned. It's said that if you see an eagle feather floating on the wind then it's a sign that these souls are close by.

Natural Wonders

Left The best way to get to the Parting of the Waters is by hiking along the Continental Divide Trail

Above left At less than a mile long, Hall of Mosses trail is ideal for hikers both young and old

Above right Daniel Boone made his name by helping to settle Kentucky in the face of fierce resistance from Native Americans

Bottom At various spots inside the cave holes in the ceiling admit shafts of light, illuminating the otherwise pitch-black depths

Parting of the Waters
CONTINENTAL DIVIDE TRAIL, MORAN, WYOMING
UTC-7

This may sound like a biblical event, but the forces that divide the water gushing down Two Ocean Pass in Wyoming's Bridger-Teton National Park are of an earthly nature. As the terrain flattens out, the waters of North Two Ocean Creek split in two, forming a pair of distributaries: Pacific Creek and Atlantic Creek. As the names suggest, these separate channels flow off towards their respective oceans. The Pacific Creek reaches its destination via two rivers – Smoke and Columbia – on a journey of 2,177 kilometres (1,353 miles) in total. Its Atlantic counterpart, meanwhile, pours into the Missouri River and then on into the mighty Mississippi, from where it eventually reaches the Gulf of Mexico, 5,613 kilometres (3,488 miles) away from its starting point.

Hall of Mosses
OLYMPIC NATIONAL PARK, FORKS, WASHINGTON
UTC-7

Hidden in the depths of the Hoh Rainforest in Washington State's Olympic National Park is a trail straight out of a fantasy book. Here towering trees draped in thick, lush moss form a vast green canopy, their shaggy limbs reaching out like the arms of gigantic creatures in a fairytale. The Sitka spruces and bigleaf maples that create this ethereal expanse of forest receive the majority of the water that sustains them during the winter months, a deluge that helps the ferns and mosses carpeting the forest floor to thrive. Those following the family friendly trail through this magical world should also be on the lookout for the majestic Roosevelt Elk and the suitably named bright yellow banana slug.

Tri-State Peak
MIDDELSBORO, KENTUCKY
UTC-5

Found in Cumberland Gap National Historical Park at an elevation of 610 metres (2,000 feet), this peak marks the point where Kentucky, Tennessee and Virginia meet. Here hikers can stand in all three states simultaneously inside a specially built pavilion. The 480-kilometre (300-mile) Cumberland Mountain Trail also begins at this location, and there is a plaque denoting the site as a Royal Colonial Boundary in 1665. Famed frontiersman Daniel Boone and four companions trekked through the Cumberland Gap in 1769 on a hunting expedition, and two Union forts were erected in the area during the bloody American Civil War of 1861-1865.

Coconino Lava River Cave
FLAGSTAFF, ARIZONA
UTC-7

Violently excavated 700,000 years ago when lava frothed out of vents in Hart Prairie, this gaping tunnel was unearthed in 1915. While the top, bottom and sides of the lava flow quickly began to cool off, the middle, which remained molten, drained away, leaving a passage in its wake that is 1.2 kilometres (0.8 miles) in length, up to nine metres (30 feet) high and features a Y-shape intersection where two separate tunnels join to become one. Parts of the cave appear to shimmer, an effect created by condensation that results from the mixture of the hot desert just above the surface and the cooler conditions underneath. The cave is open all year round and is free to access, but good walking boots and a torch are an absolute must.

Horsetail Falls Firefall
YOSEMITE NATIONAL PARK, CALIFORNIA
UTC-8

Cascading down the face of Yosemite Park's El Capitan mountain as if from the mouth of a dragon, this glowing firefall is a unique display of the perfect elements combining to create a mesmerising illusion. Flowing over the mountain's eastern face through the winter and into early spring, as the sun slips out of the day, the water appears to ignite as it reflects the fading daylight, making for a shimmering column of "fire" unlike anything else you've ever seen. Incredibly (and it must be said, rather recklessly) park workers used to engineer their own light shows by forcing mounds of lit coal over the cliff for tourists to gawp at. That was until some bright spark realised the potential of starting a forest fire and the custom was stopped.

The Mother Spring
PAGOSA SPRINGS, COLORADO
UTC-7

Nobody knows for certain just how far down the world's deepest geothermal hot spring plunges, but it's definitely over 305 metres (1,000 feet). We can be sure of this thanks to the efforts of the Guinness World Records team, who dropped a plumb line into its dark waters that reached this distance before running out. Used by humans for at least 9,000 years, the Mother Spring derives its name from the fact that it feeds several smaller springs. The springs are sacred to Navajo people, who believe that humans first clambered out of the ground near Pagosa Springs, while the Ute tribe say its waters possess healing properties.

Rainbow Bridge
NAVAJO MOUNTAIN, UTAH
UTC-7

Arcing over the shallow waters of Lake Powell, the Rainbow Bridge is the most spectacular feature of Glen Canyon National Recreation Area, a 1.25-million-acre expanse of rocks and caverns. At 88 metres (290 feet) high and 84 metres (275 feet) across, this sandstone bridge is one of the largest natural overpasses in the world. Formed by water and wind lashing it for millions of years, it was classified as a National Monument by President William Howard Taft in 1910. The canyon is also the site of a single dinosaur footprint thought to have belonged to a dilophosaurus, which, contrary to its depiction in the first *Jurassic Park* film, couldn't spit venom or deploy a neck frill.

Top left The waterfall is fed by melting snow and plunges 457 metres (1,500 feet) from the summit

Above left Wounded Civil War soldiers came to convalesce at the springs, and in the 1880s Mary Winter Fisher founded a medical practice here

Above While the curved section of the Rainbow Bridge is made of Navajo sandstone, its foundations are comprised of Kayenta sandstone

Natural Wonders

Thor's Well
YACHATS, OREGON

Time zone **UTC-8**

Below Thor's Well is also known as the drainpipe of the Pacific

Bottom This granite monolith rises to an elevation of 1,210 metres (3,970 feet)

Named in honour of the Norse god of storms, this remarkable sinkhole gives the impression that it's draining the ocean as it crashes into the coast of Oregon. Around six metres (20 feet) deep, the well likely began as a cave that was steadily eroded into existence by the pummeling waves of the North Pacific. At some point the roof of the cave imploded, creating a well. Naturally at its most volatile at high tide, Thor's Well is yet to claim a life, but it has swept plenty of people off their feet after they ventured a little too close, including a Hawaii-based photographer who came to snap the well in 2016.

TIP THOR'S WELL IS VERY DANGEROUS: MAKE SURE THAT YOU FOLLOW THE INFORMATION SIGNS AT THE SITE.

Looking Glass Rock
BREVARD, NORTH CAROLINA
UTC-5

So called for the way frozen rainwater on its smooth face reflects the sun, Looking Glass Rock hunches over Pisgah National Forest like a giant that isn't quite sure it belongs. This isolated mountain is an inselberg – a mountain that stands alone. Looking Glass Rock is also a pluton, which is formed when magma cools and solidifies beneath Earth's surface. This igneous rock is classified as intrusive as it is forced in between other rocks, where it then hardens. The process that ultimately created this unusual peak began over 390 million years ago, but it wasn't until 1966 that it was finally conquered by humans. In December of that year, Bobb Watts, Robert Gillespie and Steve Longenecker made history by scaling a crag known as the Nose. ★

THE Mysterious Marfa Lights

For more than 100 years, mysterious and colourful orbs of light have illuminated the night sky over the town of Marfa, Texas

WORDS Catherine Curzon

In 1883, cowhand Robert Ellison was herding cattle across Mitchell Flat, just east of the Texan town of Marfa, when he saw lights flickering in the darkness. He dismissed the sight as the lights from Apache campfires burning beneath the Chinati Mountains, little realising that he had made the first recorded sighting of the infamous Marfa Lights.

Ever since that night, the lights have appeared sporadically in the desert night and for the townspeople of Marfa they are just part of everyday life in the desert. Approximately the size of a football, the multicoloured orbs dance and hover, split and combine as they put on a blazing show for the thousands of spectators who flock to the area every year, hoping for a glimpse of this breathtaking phenomena. The chances are slim - there's no guessing when they'll appear and they rarely make more than a couple of dozen showings in one year - but that only makes them even more fascinating. Their colours vary between red, blue, yellow and white, but they never stay still for long.

Perhaps unsurprisingly, both the scientific and esoteric communities have attempted to find an explanation for the evening lightshow. From the scientific side, suggestions have ranged from the mundane - headlights passing on a nearby highway - to an optical illusion caused by light refraction, known as a Fata Morgana. Still others have laid the blame at the door of swamp gas, which might ignite under very specific conditions and has provided an explanation for historical will-o'-the-wisp sightings. Yet spectators claim that the orbs don't move like flames, but with an almost deliberate intent.

Paranormal fans, meanwhile, have advanced their own theories including visitors from another planet, ghostly Spanish adventurers, shapeshifters or desert spirits. Whatever the explanation, the sleepy town of Marfa has embraced its notoriety and welcomes visitors who hope to see the colourful orbs, whatever they may be. Marfa hosts its own Marfa Lights Festival and has even erected a viewing platform, where crowds gather nightly and gaze out into the darkness. Some of those crowds seek a scientific explanation for the phenomenon, others hope for the chance to meet visitors from another planet or spiritual realm, but as they look out into the sky, all of them share one aim: to experience the legendary Marfa Lights in person. ★

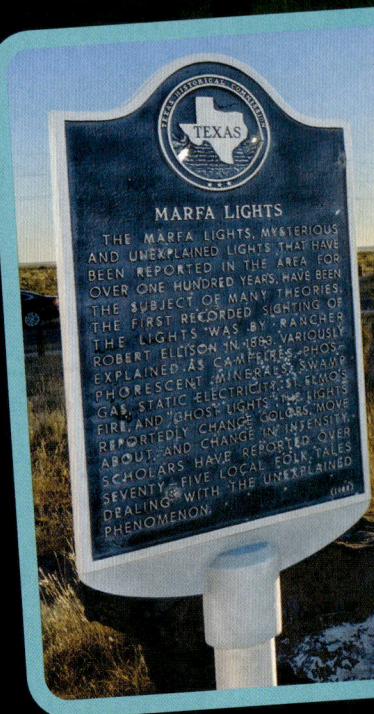

Marfa, Texas

> The size of a football, the orbs dance and hover, split and combine as they put on a blazing show

Location
Marfa, Texas
~
Time zone
UTC-6

Below Nobody can tell when the Marfa Lights will make an appearance, but whenever they do they defy explanation as they dance in the Texas darkness

Above In the apparently empty desert outside Marfa, Texas, a mysterious but compelling lightshow has been drawing skeptics and believers for decades

Right Marfa has embraced its notoriety and every night, thousands gather in the hope of catching a glimpse of the lights

Images: Alamy, Getty Images, Adobe Stock

The VOODOO-VIBED Necropolis

From dark magic and vampires to slavery, plagues and hurricanes, there are endless reasons why New Orleans is considered America's most haunted city

WORDS Alice Pattillo

Location: New Orleans, Louisiana
Time zone: UTC-5

Like much of the US, New Orleans was built upon cursed land. Founded by French-Canadian Jean-Baptiste Le Moyne de Bienbille, nobody wanted to settle in the swamp land that had formerly been occupied by the native Chitimacha, so the French shipped off their criminals to the bayou. Things have only gotten darker over its 300 year history. From murder to sinister superstitions, there are numerous reasons why it is one of the most haunted cities in the US. In fact, landlords often advertise their properties as either 'haunted' or 'not haunted' so that potential tenants know what they are in for. Without straying too far from the city's famous French Quarter, you can explore some of its spookiest spots and learn all about this bubbling cauldron of culture and superstition.

New Orleans Voodoo
FRENCH QUARTER

Louisiana voodoo is a fusion of many different belief systems including Roman Catholicism and Haitian Vodou. Initially praticised in secret, it grew considerably in popularity during the 19th century with New Orleans-based practitioners such as Marie Laveau and Doctor John. Although the practise saw a decline during the 20th century, tourism encouraged a revival and you will see numerous stores devoted to witchcraft and magic, including Reverend Zombie's House Of Voodoo, Marie Laveau's House Of Voodoo, Intuition and Esoterica Occult Goods among others, where you can enjoy a Creole bone reading, grab an authentic voodoo doll, some Marie Laveau merch and more.

To discover more about this oft-misunderstood religion, the New Orleans Historic Voodoo Museum, on Dumaine Street is an entertaining yet informative exploration of voodoo. Don't expect a professional gallery though – its artefacts and objects are rather cluttered, requiring close inspection to decipher their significance. The museum also offers walking tours to the nearby Saint Louis Cemetery Number One, psychic readings, voodoo rituals and ceremonies.

TIP
VISIT IN SPRING FOR MARDI GRAS AND BOOK A TOUR TO MANCHAC SWAMP TO SEE THE REAL LOUISIANA.

New Orleans

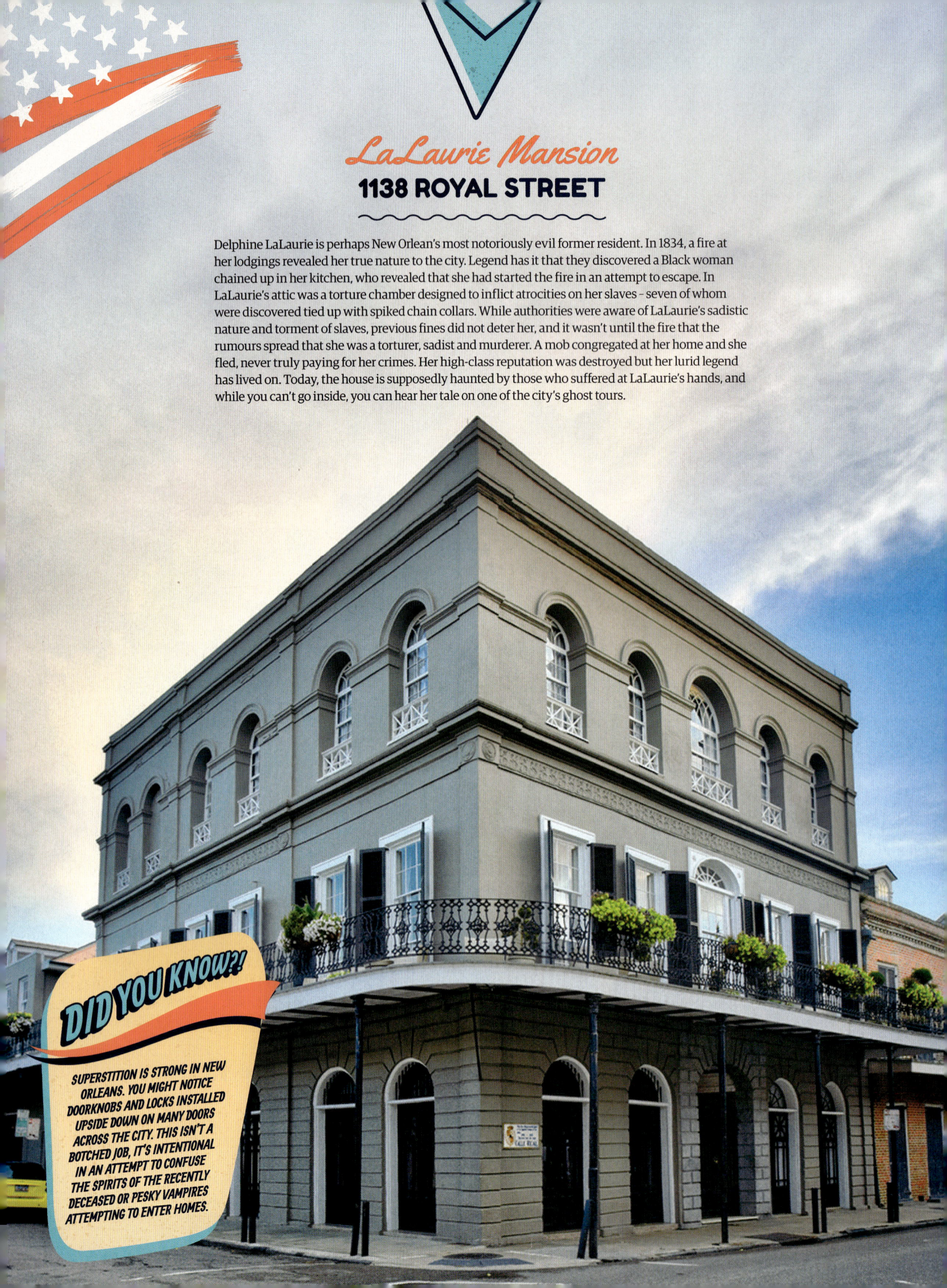

LaLaurie Mansion
1138 ROYAL STREET

Delphine LaLaurie is perhaps New Orlean's most notoriously evil former resident. In 1834, a fire at her lodgings revealed her true nature to the city. Legend has it that they discovered a Black woman chained up in her kitchen, who revealed that she had started the fire in an attempt to escape. In LaLaurie's attic was a torture chamber designed to inflict atrocities on her slaves – seven of whom were discovered tied up with spiked chain collars. While authorities were aware of LaLaurie's sadistic nature and torment of slaves, previous fines did not deter her, and it wasn't until the fire that the rumours spread that she was a torturer, sadist and murderer. A mob congregated at her home and she fled, never truly paying for her crimes. Her high-class reputation was destroyed but her lurid legend has lived on. Today, the house is supposedly haunted by those who suffered at LaLaurie's hands, and while you can't go inside, you can hear her tale on one of the city's ghost tours.

DID YOU KNOW?!

SUPERSTITION IS STRONG IN NEW ORLEANS. YOU MIGHT NOTICE DOORKNOBS AND LOCKS INSTALLED UPSIDE DOWN ON MANY DOORS ACROSS THE CITY. THIS ISN'T A BOTCHED JOB, IT'S INTENTIONAL IN AN ATTEMPT TO CONFUSE THE SPIRITS OF THE RECENTLY DECEASED OR PESKY VAMPIRES ATTEMPTING TO ENTER HOMES.

Bourbon Orleans Hotel
717 ORLEANS SREET

The Bourbon is one of the city's most haunted hotels (and there are quite a few!). Situated in the heart of the French Quarter, the hotel is haunted by the ghosts of child victims of the 19th century yellow fever pandemic, a confederate soldier and the dancing phantom of a woman. Dare to stay in the Bourbon's most haunted suite, Room 644, and you might find yourself awoken by a ghostly nun or, even more sinisterly, anguished screams.

Saint Louis Cemetery Number One
425 BASIN STREET

With New Orleans' sitting at or below sea level, the water table of the soil is extremely high – meaning the dead can't be buried traditionally six feet under, for risk of the coffin or casket winding up water-logged, or worse, being displaced from the ground and popping up to the surface. Instead, NOLA's deceased occupy above ground tombs that look like stone houses and are laid out in regular rows that resemble streets, and so the city's historic cemeteries are referred to as 'Cities of the Dead'.

Perhaps the most infamous of New Orleans cemeteries is Saint Louis Cemetery Number One, the oldest and most haunted burial ground in the city. Built in 1789, St. Louis is the permanent resting place of the Voodoo Queen of New Orleans, Marie Laveau – her grave adorned with various offerings and decorated in small Xs graffitied by those visitors who have attempted to invoke the spirit of the infamous witch for assistance. Many believe her very spirit can be seen on St John's Eve, identifiable by the knotted red hankerchief she wore around her neck. But fear not, Laveaux wasn't an evil woman, rather the opposite – her folk magic brought spiritual and physical healing to many.

New Orleans Pharmacy Museum
514 CHARTRES STREET

This 19th century former apothecary looks as it would have done 200 years ago, packed with voodoo potions, weird medicines and superstitious cures. There's also the spirit of the pharmacy's former Victorian owner, Dr Joseph Dupas, who is said to haunt the premises after closing time. Supposedly, he used to practise voodoo and perform horrific experiments on pregnant Black slave women, so make sure you swing by while the museum is open. ★

Badlands. It's a hard word for places that are among the most beautiful on the planet. But the name has a long history. It comes originally from people who knew the land more intimately than anyone else: the Native Americans. The Lakota people, who roamed the Great Plains hunting the vast buffalo herds, called the area that is now the Badlands National Park "mako sica". In English, this is 'bad lands'. The French-speaking trappers who were the first Europeans to visit the area called it "les mauvaises terres a traveser" ('bad lands to travel across'), probably taking the name both from the Lakota term and their own experiences when trying to cross these bad lands.

Geologically and climatically, badlands share some common features. They almost always occur in arid and semi-arid regions, typified by low annual rainfall but where there will usually be a few apocalyptic storms each year. Another feature of badlands are the underlying rocks: soft sedimentary rocks, such as sandstone, limestone and mudrock. These are poor in nutrients, which means that the top layer of soil will support only a thin layer of vegetation. Then, when one of those torrential rainfalls drops, the water flows into channels that rapidly erode the landscape into gullies and ravines. These drainage channels score the landscape, making it hard to navigate and harder to cross. What's more, since the surface layers are often composed of fine clay and silt, when it does rain, it turns the surface into a clinging, slippery mud which turns walking into an endurance exercise perched somewhere between wading through quicksand and slipping on ice.

This is something to bear in mind if you're visiting. Keep an eye on the weather forecast. As with most American National Parks, the vast majority of visitors don't venture more than a couple of hundred yards from the main access roads and view points. These view points will have great views but you will have to share with hundreds of other people. The writer recalls, at Yellowstone National Park near one of the mudpots, hearing visitors from all over the world imitating the sound of bursting mud bubbles using their national variation on the sound 'plop'! Very entertaining but not really an experience of the wilderness...

However, the good news is that using your feet will quickly take you away from the crowds and open out vistas that you alone are there to see. But before heading out, ensure that you plan your route and talk to the park rangers. They are the experts in the area and they are there to make sure that you don't end up getting lost and needing rescue. Listen to their advice. Having done that, get out there. You will never see anything more beautiful than these 'bad lands'.

Locations
Colorado, Montana, Nebraska, New Mexico, North Carolina, North Dakokta, South Dakota, Utah

~
Time zone
Various

The so-called badlands of the USA are anything but: they are breathtakingly beautiful

BAD but, Beautiful

America is big in a way that they just don't see in Europe.

You'll be driving to get to these badlands and, in most cases, you'll be a long way from anywhere

WORDS Edoardo Albert

TIP MAKE SURE YOU STICK TO ESTABLISHED TRAILS AND OBSERVE SAFETY PROTOCOLS AT ALL TIMES.

Toadstool Geologic Park
NEBRASKA
UTC-6

We could say Nebraska gets a bad rap but often, it just gets ignored. It doesn't even bother to put a state slogan on its number plates. At least Toadstool Geologic Park gives the visitor a reason to stop. It's a small park by American standards but the weird, erosion-carved rock formations, many of which do look like toadstools, give the park an eerie, Alice-in-Wonderland-filtered-through-American-badlands vibe. Walking the trails will also reveal many fossils still embedded in the rocks, making this a great park for amateur palaeontologists. What's more, you will likely have it pretty well entirely to yourself. So if you want to try a taste of wilderness without too much danger of getting lost, this is a good place to go.

Dinosaur National Monument
COLORADO & UTAH
UTC-7

This is the place for fossil bones, ancient art and, being Utah and Colorado, walking down into river-carved canyons in the morning and then climbing laboriously up again in the afternoon. Dinosaur National Monument covers the confluence of the Green and Yampa rivers. Their erosion revealed beds of rock littered with the fossils of dinosaurs, most memorably revealed in the excellent Quarry Exhibit Hall, which preserves a cliff studded with fossils for visitors.

Rafting on the Green River is exhilarating and provides a unique perspective upon the red cliffs towering above the river and, in summer, the water is cooling (useful given the high temperature at the bottom of the canyon).

The Native American Fremont people who lived here have left many examples of rock art which the dry climate has preserved. Some of these are easily accessed near the scenic driving routes but there are others that you will find only by walking – ask a Ranger about some of these hidden treasures.

Paint Mines Interpretive Park
COLORADO
UTC-7

By American standards, this park is tiny at only 740 acres (3 square kilometres). The advantage of this is that, if you're in the area, you can see it all in half a day. In fact, the 3.4 mile (5.5km) trail through the park can be walked in a couple of hours. Hiking it will reveal the coloured clays that Native Americans used for painting and pottery. The gullies and gulches make for a multi-coloured maze but the Native Americans also used them as channels to funnel panicking herds of buffalo into kill zones where they could slaughter them more easily. For those herds of buffalo, these really were bad lands.

Canyonlands National Park
UTAH
UTC-7

Millions of years ago, the Colorado Plateau was the flat bed to a shallow tropical sea. Then the sea dried out and the land rose – and it kept rising, until the flat plateau rose thousands of feet above sea level. Today, the average elevation of the plateau is about 6,500 feet (2,000 metres). But after it was lifted up, the soft red rock which made the plateau began to be carved out. Wind, rain and, most of all, the rivers that flowed across the plateau started cutting paths through the sandstone, carving deeper and deeper.

Canyonlands National Park preserves the confluence of the Colorado and Green rivers, and the surrounding area. Walking here is the opposite of hill walking elsewhere: you start at the top, on the surrounding plateau, and then head down into the canyons and gulches. Reaching the bottom the walking levels out but beware: the hard part, the climb out, comes at the end. Depending on how far down you went, it can be gruelling.

Canyonlands has the usual scenic drive with viewpoints but, if you can, leave the car and walk. Some advice from the writer's visits: it gets hotter as you get lower. Make sure you take lots of water and, in summer, try to start walking at dawn and rest during the hottest part of the day in the shade. For another perspective, try rafting down one or other of the rivers.

Top left: One of the excellent interpretive panels that explain to visitors what they can see at Toadstool Geologic Park

Middle top The fossilised skull of an allosaurus in the Quarry Exhibit Hall

Middle bottom Brightly coloured hoodoos displaying the coloured clays that were used by Native Americans for paint and pottery

Above The exhilaration of rafting the rapids in Canyonlands National Park has to be experienced to be believed

Opposite It's a big country

Images: Alamy

Badlands National Park
SOUTH DAKOTA

Time zone
UTC-7

Badlands National Park is the original bad land, the one that all the others were named for. Driving the Badlands Loop State Scenic Byway, which branches off from I-90, the longest interstate highway in the US, it can be hard to appreciate, particularly in the high tourist season, when you'll often be bumper-to-bumper with slow moving RVs which will brake abruptly when someone inside spots a distant brown dot and screams, "Buffalo!"

But visit when the road is quiet or, better still, park the car and hike one of the trails and then you will walk into wonderland. Badlands has eight official trails. Most of these are short, a mile or less. Only two, the four-mile Medicine Root Loop and the ten-mile Castle Trail, are at all strenuous and even these anyone of reasonable fitness should be able to walk in a day. The main danger lies in the climate: blistering in summer, frigid in winter with sudden storms possible throughout the year. Carry water, wear a hat and sunscreen.

However, if you can confidently navigate with map and compass, Badlands allows off-trail hiking. Doing this will really take you into almost completely unspoiled wilderness. But make sure you know what you're doing.

If you can, it's worth it though. This writer remembers breasting an unmarked ridge to look out over a vista of pale red ridges and shadow gorges, the sun low in the west, looking like the morning and the evening of the world, with beyond the great grass plains running to infinity. This was a glimpse of another world indeed, far from daily reality. »

TIP
VISIT THE BADLANDS PAGE AT NPS.GOV TO CHECK FOR ANY ALERTS BEFORE YOU GO.

" *Park the car and hike one of the trails and then you will walk into wonderland*

Left Imagine the impact of seeing this for the first time with no prior knowledge whatsoever

Below Makoshika State Park is one of the best places to go on the trail of dinosaur fossils

Bottom Theodore Roosevelt enthusiastically hunted buffalo but also worked for their conservation: they now have a home in the National Park named after him

DID YOU KNOW?!

BRYCE CANYON BOASTS SOME OF THE DARKEST NIGHT SKIES IN THE USA. CHECK OUT ITS ASTRONOMY TOURS AND MOON-VIEWING WALKS TO EXPERIENCE ITS MAJESTY.

Bryce Canyon National Park
UTAH
UTC-7

The writer of this feature first visited Bryce Canyon in 1989. He was driving south from Yellowstone to the Grand Canyon but an acquaintance met on the long way had said, "Stop off at Bryce Canyon." This was before the internet had been invented. His guide book contained only a brief mention of Bryce Canyon; he had never seen a picture of it nor heard of it before. So it was with a completely clear mind that he and his friends arrived at Bryce, parked their car and wandered along a trail towards what was signposted as Sunset Point. Up until then, everything seemed quite normal for the area: the flat, arid tableland of the Colorado Plateau.

And then we got to Sunset Point. Have you heard the cliché of how people's jaws will drop open in amazement? It's a cliché because it's true. Our jaws did drop open. We had never seen - never dreamed - of anything like this.

Jagged, orange cliffs, towers of sandstone red, each cliff and tower banded into layers of colour, the cliffs and towers sculpted into wild, twisted columns as if by the hand of an artist driven to madness and ecstasy by his visions.

Your writer wishes you could see it as he saw it, all those years ago, with no inkling of what he was about to see.

We spent the next few days wandering the trails of Bryce Canyon in a haze of wonder. As with all American national parks, walking will quickly get you away from the crowds and, in any case, Bryce doesn't draw anything like the crowds of its big cousin further south, the Grand Canyon. But for us, having seen Bryce Canyon, the Grand Canyon was, in comparison, a disappointment: big, yes, but vulgar in its size next to the delicate, wind and rain sculptures of Bryce.

Makoshika State Park
MONTANA
UTC-7

Makoshika is badlands, Montana style. For years, the motto on the state license plates was 'Big Sky Country' and it is. But Makoshika also has fossils - there's a good display at the visitors' centre - and dramatic badlands landscapes. In fact, there's so many fossil Triceratops there that they no longer bother excavating them. The hiking trails are excellent but none are too strenuous: the longest is five miles and it takes the walker to the Hungry Joe overlook, with its vast vista over the Yellowstone River flowing through the valley below. If you're lucky, you will spot one of the herds of wild horses that wander through the park. Seeing them will take you immediately back to the days of the Great Plains hunters.

Badlands

Bisti Badlands (De-Na-Zin Wilderness Area)
NEW MEXICO
UTC-7

Tired of driving behind convoys of RVs? Annoyed by cars blaring music in a National Park? Want true solitude and a taste, or a long draught, of genuine wilderness? Then the Bisti Badlands (also known as the De-Na-Zin Wilderness Area) is for you. The only way in is on gravel roads, there are no facilities in the park and the only water is in the jerry cans you brought in with you. But if you do make your preparations (and make sure you do, it's an unforgiving place) then you'll be rewarded with desert solitude, a silence that you've never heard before and vistas of redstone hoodoos, the weird, sculptured pillars formed by erosion. These are properly desert badlands, with very little vegetation. Animal life is sparse and shy. There are no trails so, if you set off from the trailhead you need to be able to map read, compass read, and cope with the conditions (searing in summer, freezing in winter, unpredictable in spring and autumn). It's not a place for the inexperienced but, should you visit, you won't forget it.

Ah-Shi-Sle-Pah Wilderness Study Area
NEW MEXICO
UTC-7

If the Bisti Badlands have whetted your appetite for intricately carved hoodoos and a genuine experience of wilderness, then you don't have to go far to repeat the experience: the Ah-Shi-Sle-Pah Wilderness Study Area is just over 30 miles to the south west. Like Bisti, it is a genuine wilderness area, with no facilities; bring in everything you'll need for your stay. Also like Bisti, it's blissfully free of scenic driving loops. Apart from the dirt road into the wilderness area, there are no roads. To see its wonders, such as the extraordinary hoodoo called the Alien Throne, you will need to walk. There are no marked trails and mobile coverage is poor, so you will need either map and compass or a GPS designed for hiking in order to explore safely.

Top These extraordinary rock formations in the Bisti Badlands are called the Wings

Above This remarkable area is called, quite appropriately, the Valley of Dreams

Right Snow brings a pristine beauty to the hoodoos of Cedar Breaks National Park

Theodore Roosevelt National Park
NORTH DAKOTA
North Unit UTC-6 / South Unit UTC-7

On 14 February 1884, future US president Theodore Roosevelt lost his wife and his mother within hours of each other. In his grief and shock, Roosevelt retreated to a part of the North Dakota badlands. There, amid the vast plains and under the innumerable stars, he slowly healed - and became a convinced conservationist, founding many national parks while he was president. Theodore Roosevelt National Park, named in his honour, is split into three: the larger and more visited South Unit (good for drive-by tourists); the North Unit and the Elkhorn Ranch, which preserves the site of Roosevelt's ranch (the ranch itself is long gone). Which to visit? Ideally, all three. But if you must choose, the South Unit has better access and more expansive views out over the gullies and down to the grasslands; the North Unit is more remote and wilder with more animals (although, on foot, they will spot you before you see them and likely move away). The Ranch, in between, is ranch land, with its own charm. So, three parks for the price of one.

Cedar Breaks National Park
UTAH
UTC-7

Should your visit to Bryce Canyon have whetted your appetite for astonishing geological landscapes studded with sandstone hoodoos then you're in luck. Drive 60 miles west and you'll find, in Cedar Breaks National Park, another opportunity to look down on such a landscape. In fact, because Cedar Breaks is a natural geological amphitheatre, there are natural viewing platforms from which you can see the whole extraordinary redstone bowl laid out before you.

The edge of the bowl is high, at 10,000 feet, which means it gets cold overnight even in summer and in winter there is often snow. Indeed, for many visitors, it's the winter that is most magical here, with many people arriving by snowmobile or hiking in on snowshoes.

The Stilt Village of UKIVOK

Hugging a sheer cliff side on a small island off Alaska is an abandoned town built on wooden stilts

WORDS **Jack Griffiths**

Location
King Island, Alaska
~
Time zone
UTC-8

Ukivok, Alaska

King Island or Ugiuvak sits in the Bering Strait off the coast of Alaska. The island was once home to a native population, the Iñupiat or Aseuluk, who hail from the northwest of Alaska. One of their villages, Ukivok, was built on wooden stilts and sits precariously on a cliff edge. The structures still remain there today, but its 200 inhabitants abandoned the site in the 1970s.

Perched at a 45 degree angle, the original buildings were initially constructed of a mix of walrus hide and stone but were replaced with wooden huts. The village was constructed on stilts to allow it to remain sturdy on the cliff edge. It was built in its location due to the lack of flat ground on an island that is only 3.2km (2 miles) in diameter. The isle is a stormy and rocky place and Ukivok relied on fishing and whaling in the summer and hunting crabs and seals in the winter. It's thought that it was more populous in the winter as, in the summer, the residents would travel to the Alaskan mainland to sell produce. The village is now a time capsule of a former community, still standing despite erosion from the sea and the wind.

The local population was struck with bouts of tuberculosis in the 1940s and 1950s. It was deserted two decades later after the Bureau of Indian Affairs closed the village's school, declaring that all children needed to attend school in Nome on the mainland. Its entire population migrated, leaving behind the shells of the stilted wooden huts we see today.

King Island is officially owned by the King Island Native Corporation, a community-based organisation, and anyone who wants to visits needs permission to set foot on the island. In recent years, shipping routes have ventured closer to its shores, raising concerns with former residents that tourists might try and access the village that still contains their belongings and families' heritage. There are also fears about how climate change will affect the island, with reduced ice in the Arctic fuelling more tourism and the tendency for vessels to sail closer to the Alaskan mainland. The increased traffic could affect wildlife such as walruses and seals, which are still hunted by the local population. Efforts have been made to protect the island with proposals that shipping routes steer clear of the area so Ukivok remains untouched.

> "The village was constructed on stilts to allow it to remain sturdy"

Main James Cook sailed to the island and gave it its English name, King Island, after his lieutenant, James King in 1778

Above King Island, known as Ugiuvak in the Inupiaq language, is a semi-remote island off the coast of Alaska that cis home to a forgotten town

Left Efforts have been made to return temporarily to the village so families can reacquaint themselves with the place their older relatives once called home

IF YOU GO Down TO THE Woods...

Location: Portlock, Alaska
Time zone: UTC-9

Once a bustling settlement, by the 1950s, Portlock, Alaska, was a ghost town. Did the mysterious creatures said to stalk the surrounding forests drive its people out?

WORDS **Bee Ginger**

The idyllic coastal town of Portlock, Alaska (also known as Port Chatham), was once a peaceful fishing community predominantly populated by cannery workers, miners and lumbermen of Alaskan Native or Russian descent. However, in the early 1900s, bizarre and unexplainable events began to occur, and soon rumours of terrifying creatures attacking locals swirled through its windblown streets.

Alaska is often considered to be the land of the sasquatch, or Nantiinaq. Nantiinaq comes from the Native Alaskan Dena'ina word 'nant'ina', which eerily translates as "those who steal people". Oral histories from the Native community differentiate the Nantiinaq from its North American cousin, believing these Bigfoot-like beings to have supernatural abilities. Numerous eye witnesses described a creature standing over eight feet tall, covered in dark fur and capable of killing a moose before single-handedly dragging it off into the shadows of the trees. This half-man, half-beast has long shouldered the blame for many disappearances of not only livestock but a number of locals. Giant 18-inch footprints have been discovered in fresh snow, along with tall trees ripped out of the ground by their roots. There have also been sightings of a strange entity lurking around the mine and canning factory.

In the early 1970s, an Alaskan newspaper printed a piece from a local retired teacher who told of a number of cannery workers who had ventured into the mountains to hunt for bear and dall sheep. None returned, and no trace of them was found by searchers dispatched to look for them. Months later, however, mutilated and dismembered body parts were said to have been found in the harbour lagoon, remains that were thought to have been washed down the mountainside by the rain. The wounds on these parts were not akin to those that would be inflicted by a bear.

Vanishings continued to occur until the late 1940s, and by 1949 the residents had all fled to neighbouring villages with the exception of the postmaster, who remained to brave it alone until 1951, when he too left, abandoning the town to its lonely fate.

The official story states that the inhabitants abandoned Portlock in favour of neighbouring towns that were closer to the newly built Alaska Route 1 and therefore offered improved economic prospects. Interestingly, though, it is the century-old rumours of savage man-eating giants that persist, tales that are passed down through the generations, becoming each time more vivid and unnerving.

There is talk of reviving Portlock, but will anyone be brave enough to return to the unlucky town? Will there be more disturbing incidents? And, most importantly, are the Nantiinaq still on the prowl? ★

Images Getty Images, Alamy

Portlock, Alaska

" By 1949 the residents of Portlock had all fled to neighbouring villages

Main Portlock is located south of Seldovia on the edge of the stunning Kenai Peninsula in Port Chatham Bay. The remote area can only be reached by boat or bush aircraft

Above Rotting wooden shacks and rusting metal are all that remain of Portlock

Right The town is said to have been named in honour of British naval captain Nathaniel Portlock, who found sanctuary along these shores during his expedition to Alaska in 1786

Road to

A good road trip is to be savoured. There should be no rush; no need for speed. After all, it's about exploring new lands and glimpsing sights that you've never seen before. It's about moving from one place to another, experiencing what's around, whether natural or human-made, and gaining a fresh perspective on life. In short, it's a learning process – and education can take time.

Even so, when faced with an open road, one that has barely any traffic or, come to that, much going on either side, there is a temptation to put your foot down. You may want to get to the next stage as fast as you can and relish the freedom. But that's not the best way to approach this particular road trip. Instead, it's preferable to take your time while expecting little. For this is a road trip where you are going to leave the hustle and bustle behind and encounter a different way of life.

And so it is that we introduce the Road to Nowhere, a name that may well fill you with trepidation, although it should prove exciting. It's actually US-83, a major highway that runs from north to south, starting in Canada (if you wish to embark on the whole stretch) before ending at the Gulf of Mexico. It's also about as straight a road as you could ever hope to drive (certainly given its immense length). In that sense, it's rather difficult to get lost!

You'll get a feeling of what's to come from the moment you set off from Swan River, a tiny town in Manitoba, Canada, with a population of around 4,000. At this stage, the road is referred to as the Manitoba Highway 83 and it heads south to the North Dakota border. If you do a small amount of research, you'd see it was in the news over a decade ago when a stretch of the road collapsed and created a massive sinkhole. That's since been fixed but, as you drive along, you'll soon discover there is little else to occupy your mind.

Either side of the road is countryside and farmland for as far as the eye can see and it continues that way for a long, long time. There are some turn-offs here and there but the idea is to keep going forward. You could maybe stop off at the unincorporated community of Kenville, with its smattering of buildings. Check out Asessippi Provincial Park, pass through Miniota, take a photo of the Assiniboine Riparian Forest and maybe take a rest at Melita (population of just over 1,000). Such delights, however, are few and far between.

Once in North Dakota, you can expect much of the same, although it's worth pulling up at Minot to visit the Dakota Territory Air Museum, Scandinavian Heritage Park and Roosevelt Park Zoo. You'll then be driving through the Great Plains covered in steppe, prairie and grassland in the southwestern part of the state, maybe spotting the odd moose here and there. This will also take you parallel with the Missouri River, which you'll cross north of the North Dakota capital of Bismarck.

nowhere

US-83 Highway

The US-83 highway is one of the longest, loneliest yet most poignant routes through rural America

WORDS **David Crookes**

Location
Swan River, Manitoba, Canada to Brownsville, Texas, USA
~
Time zone
Various

Opposite top Smith Falls State Park in Nebraska is home to the state's highest waterfall

Middle left You will drive through tiny towns such as Selden, Kansas, which has a population of just 189 people

Middle right The Valentine National Wildlife Refuge looks particularly desolate when viewed from above

57

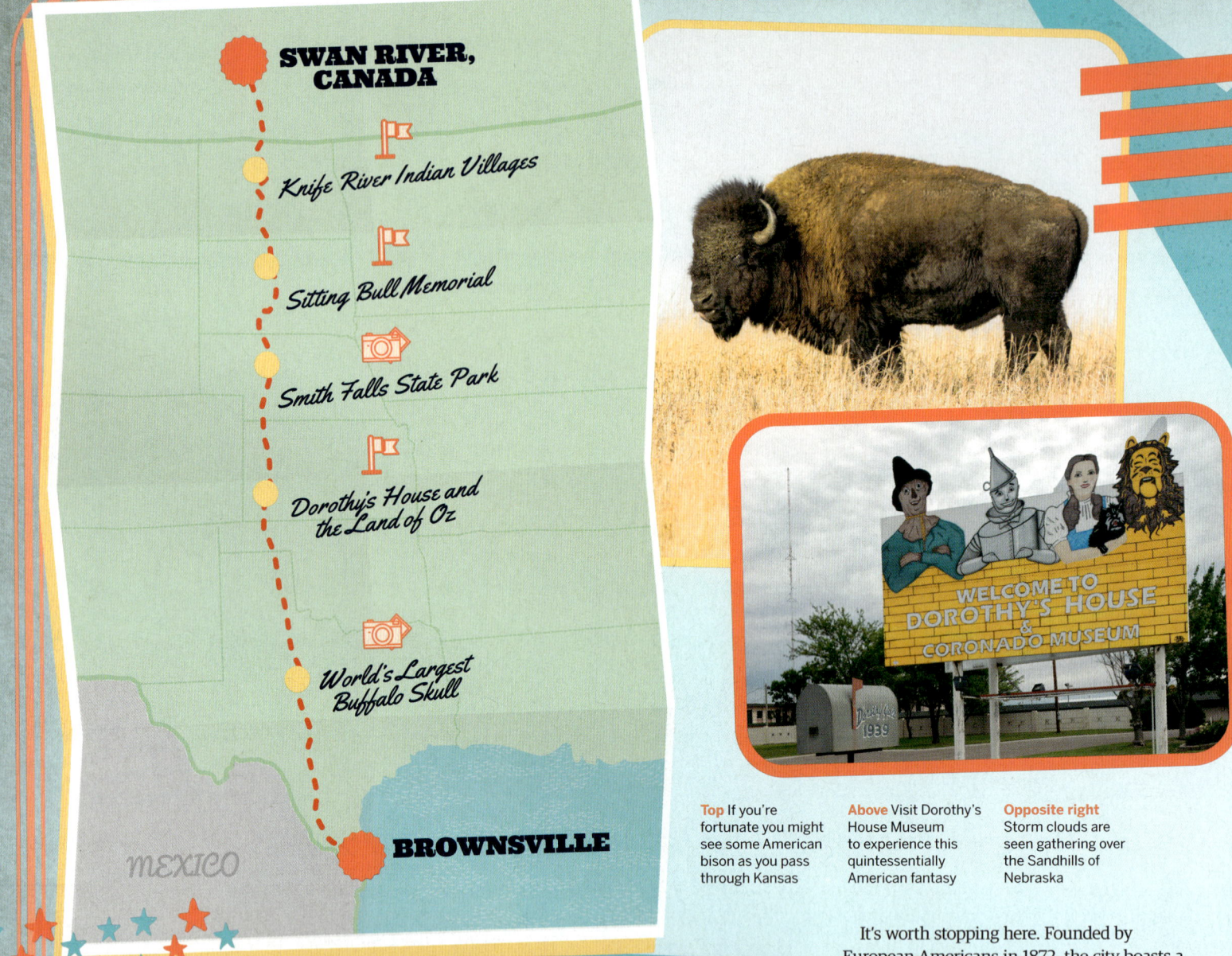

Top If you're fortunate you might see some American bison as you pass through Kansas

Above Visit Dorothy's House Museum to experience this quintessentially American fantasy

Opposite right Storm clouds are seen gathering over the Sandhills of Nebraska

It's worth stopping here. Founded by European-Americans in 1872, the city boasts a 19-storey Art Deco building and you can explore parks, the Dakota Zoo, and sights such as the Liberty Memorial and State Library. Sitting Bull, the Native American chief who was born into the Hunkpapa people and led a fight against European settlers, is buried about 160 kilometres (100 miles) away near Mobridge, South Dakota. It's marked by a monument boasting a bust created by self-taught sculptor, Korczak Ziolkowski.

Continue heading south from here and you once again come across very little for a long while before driving through the Rosebud Indian Reservation, which is home to the Sicangu Lakota Oyate people. Although the scenery in these isolated parts is breathtaking (the lush rolling prairies are dotted with small colourful canyons), life is actually tough here. Even so, people are welcoming and they will introduce you to their culture. It's part of the learning experience of remote areas such as these.

From there, you would continue south into Nebraska – incidentally, the only triple-landlocked US state. Again you'll be driving

The Knife River Indian Villages in North Dakota were home to Sacagawea before she joined the Lewis and Clark Expedition

TIP
STOCK UP WITH FOOD AND WATER WHEN YOU CAN — YOU CAN DRIVE FOR AGES BETWEEN TOWNS.

US-83 Highway

> "It makes you reflective of how the United States came to be"

PLOTTING A ROUTE

through the Great Plains while encountering cattle ranches and herds on the hillsides, given beef production is the state's largest industry. There's a feeling of peace and tranquillity in a land of rolling hills and wild sunflowers. In the heart of the Sandhills, you will also drive through the Valentine National Wildlife Refuge, with its glorious lakes and ponds.

Once in Kansas, you'll come across a large number of towns such as McCook, the capital of the Buffalo Commons, so-called because of attempts to reintroduce American bison to the area. You can also stop by at Garden City and admire its water tower, visit the Lee Richardson Zoo or maybe have some family fun in the Parrot Cove Indoor Water Park.

If you adore *The Wizard of Oz*, however, then you must pull up at Liberal, where you'll be taking a trip over the rainbow to Dorothy's House and the Land of Oz museum. Yes, it's very much a tourist destination but you'll be able to see memorabilia and take a tour.

At this stage, you're not far from crossing into Oklahoma, driving the panhandle for a brief time - the bit that makes the state look like a saucepan. This area is historically linked to slavery and it was once a lawless strip. It's also extremely hot. Within a short amount of time, you'll end up in Texas, another long drive where telegraph poles help give a feeling that you're moving forward. As before, you'll be breaking up your journey by stopping at the small towns. Fuelled and fed, you'll be in good stead to continue all the way to the Rio Grande Valley and the border with Mexico.

You will certainly look back at what will undoubtedly have been a journey unlike any others. For this isn't a road trip that takes you from city to city or from sight to sight and, as you will discover, it's all the better for it. In truth, the Wizard of Oz experience apart, you will hardly see anything that would rank high on the list of American attractions (and even Dorothy's exploits don't warrant that).

Instead, you'll be spending most of the time staring at absolutely nothing other than the road ahead, lost in your thoughts. The towns you will encounter will not be ripe for rich exploration but sparsely populated places that you often only see in made-for-TV romantic movies, where you will grab some food and engage in conversation, perhaps about beef or some other subject you never quite thought you'd be chatting about.

It makes you reflective of how the United States came to be - complete with all the struggles that go with the stage it is at today - because you're encountering a landscape largely untouched, dotted with communities that are linked, historically, to the country's earliest days. Yet, in many ways, it's also a trip that puts you in touch with people then sends you away into the wilderness, only to rinse and repeat further down the road. Sometimes boring, often exhilarating, it's an America that all too few get to see and feel. ★

US-83 has grown over time, with the original idea having been cemented by the National Highways Association in 1915. The idea was for a route running from Portal in North Dakota to Brownsville in Texas. By the next decade the Great Plains Highway was being formalised with a number (83) and it was routed through the middle of North Dakota on the insistence of the state's representatives.

Slowly but surely, US-83 began moving further south into South Dakota, Nebraska, Kansas, Oklahoma and Texas before ending up as the paved road we know today by the end of the 1950s (as opposed to the uneven rutted trail it once was). An extension north was also created, which enabled drivers to head into Canada (although not as far as Hudson Bay, as once planned). It ended up being the first paved highway between Canada and Mexico.

When car use became more prevalent, the highway was promoted by the US Canada Highway 83 Association and it issued postcards of the route. These showed the road as a way of travelling the old trails and holidaying in Canada and Mexico (reinforced by images of people fishing and taking a dip). Today it remains ideally placed to explore rural America.

Images: Getty Images, Alamy, wiki/Billy Hathorn CC BY-3.0 (route planner)

Once a year, an area of the Great Smoky Mountains begins to glow. This is not an extraterrestrial phenomenon, instead rather it's an insect's mating ritual. The culprit is a type of firefly hailing from the Elkmont region of Tennessee.

For two to three weeks between late May to early June, the lightning bugs use flashing light patterns to attract a mate. Each flash is unique to each beetle and male fireflies light up their abdomens while in flight as the females reply from the ground. It's believed that the females only respond when they are happy that enough flashing has been done by the male and reply with dimmer lights in between the male flashes. The males then fly down to the forest floor to mate with the females. As more and more fireflies join in, the flashing synchronises and soon the forest is pulsing with light in short, sharp bursts, before plunging into darkness again.

The colours are mainly greens and yellows but can also be blue or white. The vibrant display, where it looks as if a section of the forest is flickering, is caused by bioluminescence, where light is created through a chemical reaction. Unlike a light bulb, this natural occurrence

> **This area's phenomenon was once thought be unique but has also been seen in Pennsylvania**

gives off very little heat. Some fish, jellyfish and salamanders are also capable of the same feat.

This area's phenomenon was thought be unique in the Western Hemisphere but smaller displays have also been seen north east in Pennsylvania. The ritual was first recorded by Dutch travellers in 1680 in what is now Thailand and wasn't documented in the USA until 1992.

This species of firefly only live for 21 days as adults. Witnesses of the spectacle have described it as being similar to Christmas lights, a shooting star or a firework display. The beating light is difficult to catch on film and has become extremely popular with up to 8,000 people attending every year. The National Park Service limits the amount of visitors through a lottery system to not disturb the fireflies and to help preserve their habit. The service is able to predict when the display will take place by taking the temperature of the soil and then allowing for an eight-day viewing period. The sight is best seen between 9pm and midnight and in dry weather above 10 degrees Celsius (50 Fahrenheit), as too much rain, or too cool temperatures, will prevent the bugs from flashing. ★

Elkmont's Synchronised Fireflies

Tourists flock to a mountain forest in Tennessee that flickers in the darkness, all thanks to a firefly mating ritual

WORDS Jack Griffiths

Location
Elkmont, Tennessee
~
Time zone
UTC-5

Above A lottery system, where visitors have to sign up to win a pass, helps protect fireflies during their mating season

Above right The Great Smoky Mountains are part of the Blue Ridge Mountains in the Appalachians

Main Fireflies are a type of beetle that has more than 2,000 species but these are one of the few that can harmonise their light patterns

A VANISHED COLONY

The MYSTERY of ROANOKE

A 16th century English settlement on America's eastern seaboard held out great promise, and then simply disappeared. Historians have been wondering what happened ever since

WORDS **Jon Wright**

Roanoke, North Carolina

It all began so well. Walter Raleigh, always keen to swell his coffers or enhance his reputation, had managed to secure a royal patent to establish English settlements on the other side of the Atlantic. As the 1584 royal document put it, "Such remote heathen and barbarous lands, countries and territories not already possessed of any Christian prince" were ripe for the picking. Needless to say, the indigenous inhabitants of such lands saw things rather differently. But a promising start was made. In 1584, Raleigh sent two ships, under the command of Philip Amadas and Arthur Barlowe, on a reconnaissance mission. The coastal areas of present-day North Carolina seemed particularly promising, and Roanoke Island stood out as a potential hub of English colonial endeavour. The locale was far more clement than alternatives further north, such as Labrador or Newfoundland. Privateers could use it as a base from which to attack Spanish ships; forays could be made westward in the hope of tracing a route to the Pacific; the Christian message could be spread; and perhaps there might even be precious commodities about the place. As it turned out, no gold turned up, but the Brits were at least introduced to tobacco and potatoes.

One of Tudor England's great PR campaigns was swiftly launched. Barlowe returned home and talked of "goodly woods full of deer" and the "highest, reddest cedars in the world." "How profitable this land is likely to succeed," Barlowe wrote. Relations with the Native Americans which, in truth, had been strained, were cast in as positive a light as possible. An image of the jolly swapping of goods was portrayed: 50 furs in exchange for a single copper kettle, for example. The friendlier inhabitants, Barlowe recalled, "sent us every day a brace or two of fat bucks, conies, hares" and "divers kinds of fruits, melons, walnuts." Barlowe was distressed by the region's religious habits but did his best to make things sound idyllic: no better way to drum up further investment. Better yet, two quasi-ambassadors, Manteo and Wanchese, eminent members of a local tribe, travelled back to England and caused quite the stir.

In 1585, a second, more substantial expedition was launched, under the command of Richard Grenville (Raleigh, while always the backer of the project, never took the trouble to visit). 600 or so people - mostly soldiers, but also a fair few craftsmen - set up camp, and fortifications began. Again, great strides were made, with the scientist Thomas Harriot delving into the region's flora and fauna, and the painter John White producing some admirable maps and pictures. His watercolours would help to define European understandings of North America for generations to come. Unfortunately, loss of supplies en route meant that the would-be colonists were in a rather precarious position, so dealings with local tribes were of great importance. These did not progress terribly well, however, and while some useful relationships were certainly established, the situation

Location
Roanoke, North Carolina
~
Time zone
UTC-4

> *All manner of clues have cropped up through the years, but none are conclusive*

Top left Walter Raleigh, the man behind the Roanoke adventure

Above left Elizabeth I, patron of many overseas ventures, Roanoke included

Above Did the mysterious inscriptions left behind point to the colonists leaving for nearby Crotoan? And if so, why was there no trace of them to be found there?

- in general - shifted from frosty to hostile. 'Who were these English interlopers spreading disease?' appears to have been the entirely reasonable party line. For their part, the English settlers became increasingly brutish.

Grenville thought it best to flee the scene and engage in a spot of much more profitable privateering, leaving Ralph Lane and a hundred soldiers to sustain a presence at Roanoke. Matters deteriorated further so, soon enough, just a handful of troops were entrusted with the task of sustaining an English presence. The lack of a deep water port also made Roanoke a less attractive proposition than it had first seemed. Aims had now shifted, so perhaps it was wiser to seek a haven elsewhere, with Chesapeake Bay at the head of the list. Grenville stopped by following Lane's departure, finding nothing more than a few bones of a dead soldier. This was not the end of the story, however.

In 1587, John White led a third expedition. The goal was to head to the Chesapeake, but the mission stopped off at Roanoke to assess the situation. After heated arguments, an odd decision was made. White, appointed governor, and his 117 fellow travellers would once more labour to establish a Roanoke colony. It did not go well, with one of White's advisers, George Howe, being found dead in the woods, impaled with 16 arrows. The colonists returned the favour, and a catalogue of mishaps and misunderstandings ensued.

In the hopes of securing supplies and support in England, White traversed the Atlantic. This proved to be a case of bad timing. What with the Spanish Armada and blocked sea routes, White's return to America was delayed. When he finally made the trip, in 1590, he found an entirely deserted settlement at Roanoke. This was quite the mystery, and it did not take long for the speculation to begin. The letters 'CRO' were found carved on a tree, and the word 'Croatoan' had been inscribed on a post. This fitted with the idea of a prearranged signal being left behind by the colonists if they had moved on. If they had been forced to decamp, they would also leave the sign of a cross. White saw no cross, so he was hopeful that the colonists were still alive somewhere. But where? The obvious candidate was Croatoan - an island named for a local tribe (present-day Hatteras Island), which the inscriptions seemed to point to - but White was obliged to sail home, and never had the opportunity to test his theory. Various attempts were made to solve the puzzle: an expedition in 1603, for example, and various missions following the establishment of the Jamestown colony in 1607. But 400 years later, we simply cannot be sure of what happened.

Some have suggested, with not an ounce of proof, that the Spanish arrived and destroyed the Roanoke colony; others wonder if the colonists decided to risk a sea voyage home and sank without trace. Perhaps the locals simply decided to massacre them. The most intriguing, and perhaps the most plausible, notion is that the colonists, stranded and living through (as climate history suggests) a truly awful spell of weather, opted to assimilate themselves into the local population. The trouble is, any number of potential new homes have been suggested.

All manner of clues have cropped up through the years, but none of them are conclusive. Archaeological work has found English items in various places - but is this evidence of the Roanoke people's presence, or just the result of trading goods? Stone buildings, alien to the indigenous tribes, have been located. A hint that some ex-Roanoker was in residence? Various Native American groups have suggested that some of their folk are the descendents of the

Roanoke, North Carolina

exception, these artefacts are fakes. Theories have stretched to the limits of the bizarre – even cannibalism has been suggested – but historians continue to grapple with the mystery. A recent highlight was the discovery of a sign on a map, hidden beneath a patch and only visible via back-lighting, that may have indicated the presence of a resettled fort 80 kilometres (50 miles) or so from Roanoke. Perhaps that's where they, or some of them, ended up. Or perhaps, in multiple groups, they ingratiated themselves with more than one tribe and were caught up in conflicts and blotted out.

It is, one suspects, a puzzle that will one day be solved. After all, the archaeological digs continue. But the 'not knowing' has had a phenomenally important impact on US culture ever since. Almost every American schoolchild is likely to be able to tell you something about Roanoke. It is a puzzling story: one of everything going terribly wrong. Thomas Harriot, who was there from the start, wrote of all that Roanoke had to offer. He talked of otters, pearls and sugar cane, of alum on the coastline, and "a kind of grass in the country upon the blades whereof there groweth very good silk in the form of thin glittering skin." Quite the paradise but, whatever the specifics, perhaps one of the reasons the English lost out was that they behaved badly towards the people who had lived there for many centuries. ★

TIP
TODAY ROANOKE IS A POPULAR TOURIST DESTINATION, SO BOOK AHEAD TO VISIT ITS ATTRACTIONS.

Roanoke colonists, but this still remains in the category of oral, unverifiable history, despite the efforts of modern DNA science to pin things down. False leads are also abundant: notably the so-called Dare Stones, named for Eleanor Dare, the daughter of John White, marked with inscriptions that purported to tell the tale of what transpired in the 1580s. They talk of slaughter and a handful of survivors, but today most scholars believe that, with one possible

Above right The Dare Stones were purportedly inscribed by Eleanor Dare, mother of Virginia Dare, to tell her family where the colonists had gone

VIRGINIA DARE AND THE CREATION OF A MYSTERY

FEW FIGURES BETTER ENCAPSULATE THE AMERICAN FASCINATION WITH WHAT HAPPENED AT ROANOKE THAN VIRGINIA DARE

There are people in the past about whom we know a great deal. Others are almost entirely lacking when it comes to biographical detail. Virginia Dare is solidly in the latter camp, but this has not diminished her extraordinary influence in American culture. She was the granddaughter of the colony's governor, John White, and it is often suggested that she was the first child of English ancestry ever to be born (1587) in New England. Along with all the other Roanoke settlers, she had vanished by the time White returned in 1590, but her mystique has proven to be addictive. Dare has been used as an advertising symbol for everything from candy to wine. She has been perceived as a model of female fortitude, as the ultimate proto-American and, much less happily, her image has been recruited by an alarming number of bigoted groups. During the Civil Rights era, racists claimed her as a symbol of supposed racial purity – an abomination that continues to this day – and those who oppose immigration are apt to invoke her name, which has to be silly, since her parents travelled across an ocean to Dare's birthplace. Dare has been the subject of countless films and novels and, in her way, captures the frustrating uncertainty of the Roanoke mystery.

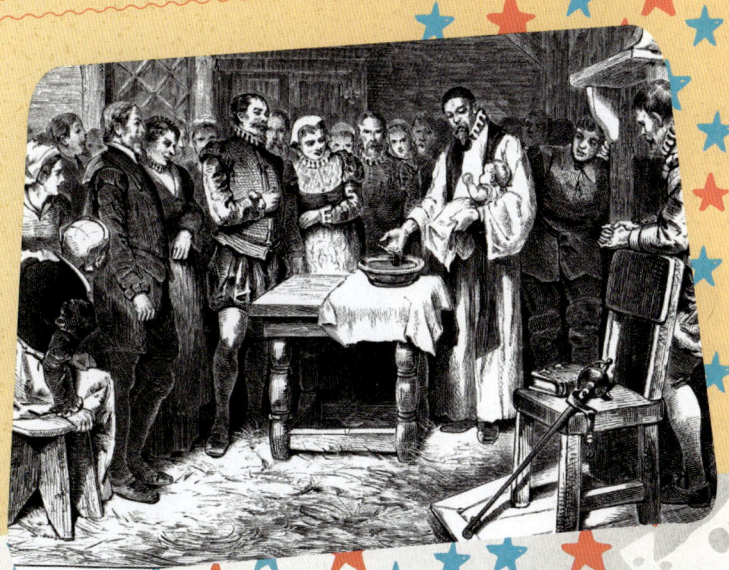

PECULIAR PENINSULAS &

From isolated lake islets to tropical keys, the states are home to numerous archipelagoes that boast some weird and wonderful sites to explore

WORDS Alice Pattillo

DID YOU KNOW?!

THE USA (INCLUDING ITS TERRITORIES OUTSIDE THE 50 STATES) HAS A WHOPPING 18,617 ISLANDS! WHILE SOME ARE TINY, AN INCREDIBLE 10,000 ARE INHABITED.

Humans love an island. Who doesn't occasionally fantasise about escaping to an uninhabited land, completely isolated from the dangers and the dramas of the rest of the world? The safety and solitude of a space completely surrounded by water where you have liberty to make your own rules sounds like a romantic dream to some – why else do celebrities buy them?

There is something magical about islands and the United States is packed with them. In fact, the US has over 18,000 islands within its territories. With the country spanning the entire width of the North American continent, from the Pacific to the Atlantic Ocean, boasting approximately almost 95,500 miles of shoreline, almost 3,800,000 square miles of land and nine distinct climates, it has a wide and varied geological history. Giant sheets of ice once covered almost the entire continent. When these glaciers melted, they carved out the Great Lakes along the eastern border with Canada. Along its extensive coastline, hurricanes, waves and tidal action have forged

IDIOSYNCRATIC ISLANDS

Islands

Locations
California, Florida, Georgia, Maryland, Maine, Massachusetts, Michigan, New York, North Carolina, Ohio

the East and Gulf Coast's barrier islands from Florida up to Maine and west to Texas. Tectonic plate activity has resulted in the West Coast's Channel Islands and San Juan Islands, volcanic eruptions created the likes of Alaska and Hawaii and river deltas have etched the likes of the Keneenaw Peninsula in Michigan and the Driftless Area of the Upper Mississippi River. The United States is also home to the world's smallest inhabited island - dubbed Just Room Enough Island, it features a house, tree, shrubs and a bench, and is located in Alexandria Bay (NY), within the Thousand Islands archipelago of 1,864 islands that stretch 50 miles from Canada to New York State.

Along with thousands of natural islands, there are hundreds that were man made: some constructed thousands of years ago by native tribes, others forged in the last few centuries, as defensive fortifications, military test sites, shipping accesses, and even (at least in the case of San Francisco's Treasure Island) to hold a world's fair.

Whether artificial or natural, surrounded by sea or fresh water, read on to discover some of the most intriguing and unique islands the United States has to offer.

The world's smallest inhabited island, Just Room Enough Island, also known as Hub Island, is essentially a house on water

Image Alamy

Portsmouth
NORTH CAROLINA
UTC-5

Located along North Carolina's Outer Banks, Portsmouth was once a bustling port. A vital point of entry for cargo travelling across the Atlantic in post-Revolutionary America, Portsmouth Village was one of the largest settlements in the area during the 1770s and continued to grow into the 19th century. Merchant ships would stop at the village's port, where enslaved men transferred their cargo into shallow draft boats in a process called lightering. However, during the Civil War of the 1800s, many residents fled to the mainland. By the 1800s, fishing had replaced shipping as the primary employment. By the mid-20th century, it had become a ghost town. Hurricane destruction, isolation and the Great Depression all contributed to the village's decline and in 1971 its final two residents, Elma Dixon and Marian Babb, left for the mainland. Since 1976 it has been on the National Register of Historic Places, and the National Park Service has maintained the site ever since. Facilities are limited, but volunteers staff the Theodore and Annie Salter House (now the Visitor Centre), the school, post office, general store and US life-saving station from mid-April to late October.

Disney's Discovery Island
BAY LAKE, FLORIDA
UTC-7

Disney purchased this small private island in Bay Lake in 1965 before the construction of Walt Disney World in Orlando. Opened as Treasure Island on 8 April 1974, the 11.5-acre island was intended as a zoological park where visitors could observe wildlife, later changing its name to Discovery Island. Home to exotic animals such as lemurs, flamingoes, giant tortoises, scarlet ibis and cranes, Discovery Island was inhabited by the last known dusky seaside sparrow, until it died and its species was declared extinct in July 1987. The resort permanently closed its doors to the public exactly 25 years after its opening, on 8 April 1999, relocating all animals to the nearby Animal Kingdom Theme Park, which had opened a year before. For over 25 years, the site has been left to be reclaimed by the natural world, abandoned with no signs of development. The island is off limits to the public, but can be seen from nearby Disney destinations such as Wilderness Lodge, Contemporary Resort, Fort Wilderness and Walt Disney World Monorail System.

Deer Island
BOSTON, MASSACHUSETTS
UTC-5

Despite being home to the second-largest sewage treatment plant in the United States, today, Deer Island is a scenic spot and a popular part of Boston Harbour Islands National Recreation Area. But its role as an exportation zone for human waste is a dark reflection of Deer Island's history, when instead of receiving human excrement, the island became a dumping ground for human bodies. In 1847, two years into Ireland's Great Famine, around 25,000 hopeful Irish refugees travelled to Boston in the hope of finding a better life for themselves. Arriving in dark, cramped vessels known as "coffin ships" thanks to their miserable conditions, it's no surprise that thousands were infected with 'ship fever' upon disembarking. Fearing an epidemic, Boston city officials quarantined the sick on Deer Island, where a hospital was established and admitted 4800 people between 1847 and 1850. 850 patients succumbed to the sickness and were buried in unmarked graves across the island. When construction crews discovered the bodies in 1990, the local Irish-American community began rallying to give them the respect they deserved. After almost 30 years of fighting for justice, the Great Hunger Memorial – a 16 feet tall Celtic cross that overlooks the harbour – was erected in their memory. The island is also home to another memorial, devoted to the Nipmuc Native Americans who were left to perish during King Philip's War (1675-1678), where their descendants pay their respects and hold a ceremony every October.

Top left The Henry Pigott House was the last occupied house on Portsmouth Island, abandoned in 1971 and now part of the historic district

Above The Great Hunger Memorial was officially dedicated to those who died during the Irish Great Famine in 2019

Left Discovery Island lies abandoned, but urban explorers beware – trespassers are prohibited!

Opposite right Mound Key was an important site of the Calusa tribe and was formed with shell, fish and pottery debris

Opposite bottom This inconspicuous island hosted a rather high-profile guest in the early 20th century

Esopus Island
STRAATSBURG, NEW YORK
UTC-5

Follow the Hudson River 84 miles from its estuary into the Atlantic Ocean in New York City and you'll discover a small uninhabited island. Esopus Island can be reached only by boat and is a popular scenic camping location. But at the dawn of the 20th century the island hosted one particular – and peculiar – camper, known to some as The Beast. Infamous occultist Aleister Crowley sought sanctuary on Esopus in 1918 in order to translate the 4th century Chinese philosophical text, *Tao Te Ching*. Living much like a mystic hermit, Crowley canoed to the island with very little food – reportedly claiming the crows would feed him – but plenty of red paint. For 40 days and 40 nights, Crowley meditated and painted Thelemic graffiti on the island's rocks. Friends and followers visited him and brought him food and other, more illicit, substances, prompting Crowley to claim he experienced visions of his past lives – in all of which he was nothing but successful and influential figures including the magician Eliphas Levi and Renaissance Pope Alexander VI. While Crowley's graffiti is unfortunately no longer visible, his monastic retreat to the island made a more permanent mark in local lore.

TIP
YOU CAN VISIT AND CAMP ON ESOPUS ISLAND, BUT IT HAS NO BATHROOM FACILITIES!

Mound Key
ESTERO BAY, FLORIDA
UTC-5

Now an archaeological state park, Mound Key is a man-made island created over 2000 years ago, by the shell mound-building ancestors of the indigenous Calusa tribe. The Calusa people built a remarkably sophisticated society centered around fishing, with the sea as their primary resource. Their power and influence spanned from Tampa Bay to Ten Thousand Islands and Mound Key is believed to have been the site of their kingdom's capital, Calos. Archaeologists have unearthed a city similar in stature to Aztec city-states on Mound Key and believe the island and its surrounding areas would have been home to around 4000 people. It was also the location of one of the original Native-European cross-culture feasts, 55 years prior to the first Thanksgiving dinner between the Wampanoag tribe and European colonists was held in Massachusetts in 1621. After Spanish conquistador Juan Ponce de León sailed to Mound Key in 1521 and wound up dead, the Europeans gave the area a wide berth until 1566, when the governor of La Florida, Pedro Menéndez de Avilés sat down with Calusa King Caalus for a lavish feast. Hosted near present-day Fort Myers, in a wooden, thatched-roof great hall large enough to accommodate 2000 people, the intent was to secure an alliance between the Spanish and the Calusa. King Caalus's sister was betrothed to Menéndez, plans were made to build a Spanish fort on Mound Key and guests dined on fish, oysters, wine and Spanish imports. It was also one of the first guitar concerts to be held upon American soil, with Spanish musicians providing entertainment. Unfortunately the alliance fell apart within a year. The Spanish killed Caalus in 1567 and his successor, Felipe, in 1569. While the Europeans were driven out not long after and the Calusa held their seat on the island until the early 1700s, their kingdom declined, with many falling victim to European diseases, brutality or enslavement.

Fort Montgomery
LAKE CHAMPLAIN, ROUSES POINT, NEW YORK
UTC-7

Fort Montgomery is located on a man-made island within Lake Champlain, the legendary home of Champ, a five-feet-long serpentine monster with impenetrable scales. A fortress was initially built here in 1816 to defend against Canada. Known as "Fort Blunder", it was inadvertently built in Canadian territory, due to a surveying error. The first fort was consequently scrapped and after some border adjustments Fort Montgomery was built to the east of the original in 1844. Once an impressive structure, some 48 feet high with a moat with drawbridge and emplacements for 125 cannons on three storeys, today it is owned and operated by the state of New York and functions as a museum.

Dry Tortugas
MONROE COUNTY, FLORIDA
UTC-5

Now one of the USA's most remote and least visited national parks, conquistador Juan Ponce de León named these Floridian islands Las Tortugas - Spanish for 'The Turtles' - in honour of the creatures that made these large clusters of coral reefs their home. The islands earned the epithet 'Dry' due to the distinct lack of freshwater in the area. The location of the islands, 70 miles west of the Florida Keys, between the Gulf of Mexico and the Atlantic Ocean, meant they became a busy shipping route. However, the corridor proved treacherous thanks to its shallow waters and unpredictable weather, leading to it being dubbed the "ship trap". The remains of numerous 17th century merchant vessels still lie beneath the waters. Garden Key Island is home to Fort Jefferson, built in 1847 to combat the infamous pirates of the Caribbean. The fortress is one of the largest coastal forts ever built. In 1935, President Roosevelt registered it as a National Monument and today it houses a museum and bookstore. The Dry Tortugas can be accessed via boat or seaplane and there is a daily ferry from Key West.

Carnegie Mansion Ruins
CUMBERLAND ISLAND, ST MARY'S, GEORGIA
UTC-7

Cumberland Island, situated off the southernmost coast of Georgia, is home to the ruins of a sprawling 19th century estate once belonging to Thomas Carnegie, the younger brother of Scottish-American industrial tycoon Andrew Carnegie. Called Dungeness, it was built with pools, a golf course and 40 smaller buildings to house 200 servants. Unfortunately, Thomas died before the estate could be completed but his widow Lucy and their nine children moved in once it was finished and remained there until the Great Depression. In 1959, a fire broke out at the abandoned home, leaving the mansion, pool house and gardens in ruins. The majority of the island is now preserved by the National Park Service as part of Cumberland Island National Seashore. Lucy had additional estates built on the island for her children, including Greyfield (now a private inn, still under the Carnegie Family's ownership), Plum Orchard (donated to the National Park Service in 1972 and available to tour) and Stafford Mansion (still privately owned by the Carnegie Family).

Fort Carroll
DUNDALK, BALTIMORE, MARYLAND
UTC-5

Built before the Civil War as a naval defence to protect the city of Baltimore, Fort Carroll was rendered obsolete before it was even finished. This man-made island was constructed in the shallow waters of Soller's Point Flats to house the hexagonal fortress, which was intended to be armed with 225 cannons. Upon the outbreak of the Civil War in 1861, only five gun platforms were ready with only two armed. By the Spanish-American War in 1898, its gun batteries were outdated and construction commenced on three modern concrete gun emplacements. But the war was already over when they were completed in September 1900. Following World War I, all the guns were removed from the fort and by 1921 the military had abandoned it. Today, Fort Carroll has become a park and bird sanctuary.

Top left Fort Montgomery State Historic Site's visitor centre is orientated to give day trippers a "gun sight" down the Hudson river

Left Once a fortress to combat the infamous pirates of the Caribbean, today Dry Tortugas is a national park well worth a visit

Top The skeletal remains of the once grand Dungeness Mansion

Above Poor Fort Carroll barely saw any action

Opposite Beaver Island is the largest island in Lake Michigan, and there are plenty of beavers, but no more Strangites

Beaver Island
LAKE MICHIGAN, MICHIGAN

Today Beaver Island is home to around 600 residents, but back in 1847 only a few hundred people inhabited it - Anishinaabeg tribal members and Irish immigrants, trading lumber, fur and fish. That was the year something strange happened - a man known as Strang arrived on the island with a small group of followers. Within three years, he had declared himself "King of the Kingdom of God on Earth" and attracted 2500 new residents. Strang's kingdom would only last six years, but the legacy of Beaver Island's Mormon pirate king would live on.

Born in New York in 1813, and a member of the Church of Jesus Christ of Latter Day Saints, Strang claimed he was guided by angels. Within the six years Strang 'ruled' the island, his followers building roads, homes and farms and attempting to convert the Irish and Native islanders to the Mormon faith. However, the Strangites garnered a negative reputation and were branded "pirates" and blamed for a string of robberies plaguing Lake Michigan. Strang himself was accused of stealing his followers' wives, violently punishing them, and sacrificing animals. In 1856 as Strang stepped onto the dock of the USS Michigan to enjoy dinner with its captain he was ambushed and shot by two of his own men, succumbing to his wounds two weeks later in Wisconsin.

Time zone: UTC-5

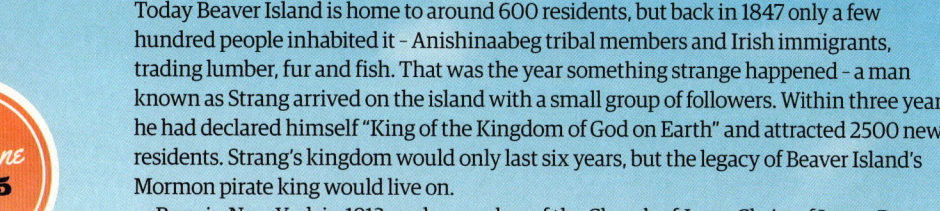

> "A man known as Strang arrived on the island with a small group of followers"

TIP
RESIDENTS SAY SPRING AND FALL ARE THE BEST TIMES TO VISIT, RATHER THAN SUMMER.

DID YOU KNOW?!
THE WATERS NEAR BEAVER ISLAND ARE RUMOURED TO BE THE LAST RESTING PLACE OF THE WRECK OF THE LOST 17TH CENTURY SHIP LE GRIFFON, LOST IN A SUDDEN STORM.

DID YOU KNOW?!

KELLEYS ISLAND IS HOME TO INSCRIPTION ROCK, A LARGE LIMESTONE BOULDER WHICH WAS CARVED WITH PETROGLYPHS BY ANCIENT NATIVE AMERICANS.

Buckle Island
NORTHWEST OF SWANS ISLAND, MAINE
UTC-5

This small uninhabited island accessible by boat from Swans Island feels like somewhere Gulliver would stumble upon his travels. Head from the beach to one of the hiking trails and your walk will be filled with whimsy. Scattered throughout the luscious woodlands are what look like fairy houses and other eccentric organic structures, eco-friendly signatures left behind by creative former visitors. The most famous piece of their art is the green-painted wooden door that marks the threshold between the dense thickets of the forest to a bright clearing.

Mackinac Island
LAKE HURON, MICHIGAN
UTC-5

Back in 1898, Mackinac Island Village Council outlawed the use of motorised vehicles. But unlike the many other municipalities who resisted the new technological advancements at the time, it maintained its prohibition of cars "within the limits of the village of Mackinac" and remains the last in the United States to still enforce a ban on automobiles (today emergency vehicles are permitted). The lack of traffic has helped to preserve its scenic tranquility and quaint charm. Over 80 per cent of the island is designated Mackinac Island State Park and the entire island is preserved as a National Historic Landmark thanks to its number of buildings of historic significance, which have undergone extensive preservation and restoration. Head to the island's Historic Downtown to discover a variety of architectural styles spanning 300 years.

Misery Islands
SALEM AND BEVERLY, MASSACHUSETTS
UTC-5

Great Misery Island and the smaller Little Misery Island allegedly gained their name after ship builder Robert Moulton was stranded on them in the 1620s during a winter storm, describing it as miserable. The eerie ruins of Misery Island Club, once a luxury resort, can be found on Great Misery along with the charred remains of early 20th century summer cottages - most business ventures upon Misery have failed. Today the islands function as a nature reserve and is open to the public for recreational activities.

Top left Feel free to create your own organic artwork, but please don't litter!

Above Escape city car fumes and stay an independent B&B – there are no chain hotels on the island, but don't worry, they still have WIFI!

Left It's really not that miserable on the Misery Islands, unless you plan on starting a business...

Islands

Above Kellys Island is home to the Glacial Grooves State Memorial

Top right Foreign sounding accents, plenty of history and uncrowded, golden beaches — you'll feel like you're in Europe

Bottom The notorious former maximum security penitentiary has a complex history

Kelleys Island
LAKE ERIE, ERIE COUNTY, OHIO
UTC-5

The village of Kelleys Island occupies the entire island of the same name, located within Lake Erie, Ohio, and despite being just shy of four and a half square miles, it has a fascinating and colourful history. The island is home to the largest and most accessible glacial grooves in the world, eroded into the Devonian limestone and dolomite approximately 18,000 years ago when ice covered the majority of North America. Found in Glacial Grooves State Memorial, now a National Natural Landmark, the limestone grooves contain fossils of extinct marine organisms. Aside from its geological wonders, Kelleys Island is home to some unique relics of human history. Prior to the Napa Valley dominating in the US wine market, the Ohio Valley ruled the industry. Early European settlers found its climate mirrored that of the Rhine, making it the perfect place to grow grapes. After war and vine disease in the valley, the epicentre of Midwestern wine production moved to Kelleys Island for a while. The remains of the two island wineries can still be found on the island.

Ocracoke
OUTER BANKS, NORTH CAROLINA
UTC-5

There are at least 30 different American-English dialects and numerous regional accents across the United States. However, while most are recognisable, there is one rare American dialect that you'd be hard pressed to place, and it's not even considered American – despite its origins arguably being more rooted in American soil than any other. Surviving solely through a small number of residents of an isolated North Carolinian island, the Ocracoke brogue doesn't appear to have evolved much since the 1600s. Known as "Hoi Toider," this entirely unique manner of speaking is a mishmash of 17th century Irish and Scottish brogues, Elizabethan English, pirate slang and Native American vernacular. But it's not just the extraordinary English variant that makes the island of Ocracoke offbeat. In fact, the whole place is unique having maintained its old-worldly spirit; with independent retailers and family-owned businesses dominating the island, you'll feel like you stepped back to simpler times.

Alcatraz
SAN FRANCISCO BAY, CALIFORNIA
UTC-8

Most infamous for its role as a federal prison where it housed numerous notorious criminals including mob boss Al Capone, Alcatraz Island has a longer and more varied history than you may think. Also known as "the Rock", its name is derived from "La Isla de los Alcatraces" (Spanish for "The Island of the Pelicans") and it is home to the oldest operating lighthouse on the West Coast, built in 1846. From 1868 to 1934 it functioned as a long-term military prison facility, and then as a federal prison until 1964. From November 1969 to 1971, Alcatraz island was occupied by a Native American group of political activists named Indians of All Tribes. The island was classified as abandoned surplus federal land at the time, spurring the activists to attempt to reclaim it. The occupation drew support from celebrities including Marlon Brando and Jane Fonda who both visited the island. The occupation brought national attention to indigenous issues, shifted federal policies regarding Native rights and established Unthanksgiving Day, held annually on the island. Today, the island is open to the public as a museum and it can be reached by ferry from Pier 33 in San Francisco.

Location
Key West, Florida
~
Time zone
UTC-5

OVERSEAS HIGHWAY

From Miami to Key West, this scenic route will offer up the best views of America's East Coast

WORDS *Jessica Leggett*

Often referred to as the 'Highway that Goes to Sea', the Overseas Highway is one of the most beautiful scenic drives in the United States, offering up incredible views of the Florida Keys and its famous turquoise waters. It is part of US Route 1 and runs from Miami all the way down to Key West.

The Overseas Highway consists of 42 connecting bridges, joining hundreds of small islands that make up the Florida Keys archipelago. It was first opened in 1938 and built on the foundations of the Florida East Coast Railroad, which was destroyed by a hurricane in 1935. In 1982, 37 of the bridges were replaced to give them much wider spans.

The route usually takes around three to four hours in one go, but there are so many locations to stop at along the way that you can easily extend your road trip to several days if you wish. Before setting off on your journey from Miami, try to spare some time to explore the city itself and enjoy its world-famous nightlife and culinary scene.

From Miami, make your way down to Key Largo, which is the first of the Florida Keys. Here, it is worth going on a diving or snorkelling excursion, as Key Largo is home to some of the country's best coral reefs. If you are interested in the coral reefs, then make sure you visit the John Pennekamp Coral Reef State Park, the first underwater preserve in the US, which can be found at mile marker 102.5. While you are at Key Largo, why not grab dinner at the Caribbean Club? The oldest bar in the Upper Keys, it appeared in the 1948 film *Key Largo*, starring Humphrey Bogart and Lauren Bacall.

As you continue on the journey, you will reach a group of tiny islands collectively known as Islamorada, Spanish for 'purple isle'. Relax at white sandy beaches and bask in the clear blue waters of the Keys.

While there are a number of different activities to keep you busy in Islamorada, arguably the most iconic landmark is Robbie's Marina. Regularly cited as one of the best locations to visit in the Florida Keys, explore local shops, go tarpon feeding and fill up on fresh seafood at the Marina. For those who like to support local artists, head to the Morada Way Arts & Cultural District, a downtown community in Islamorada, where you will discover several galleries, studio spaces and restaurants to explore.

The next group of islands along the route is called Marathon, which is home to the famed Seven Mile Bridge that is surrounded by blue water. Another unmissable part of the route, which has been featured in several films and television shows, including *2 Fast 2 Furious*, it joins the Knights Key - located in the Middle Keys - with Little Duck Key in the Lower Keys. There are actually two bridges, one for pedestrians and cyclists built in 1912, and one for vehicles built in 1982.

Located off of the old Seven Mile Bridge is Pigeon Key, a small island that is known for its historic buildings. Once the home to hundreds of workers who built the original railroad, today the island is home to eight buildings on the National Register of Historic Places, and if you would like to learn more about them, there are tours available.

Main The Overseas Highway is one of the world's most scenic drives

Middle left Hemingway House is a museum in Key West

Middle right There are a range of activities to enjoy at Robbie's Marina

Below An image of the Spiegel Grove shipwreck in Key Largo

TIP TO AVOID HURRICANE SEASON, VISIT BETWEEN DECEMBER & MAY.

THE FLORIDA REEF

Throughout your trip along the Overseas Highway, you will find many opportunities to learn about the marine wildlife of the Florida Keys. In fact, the Florida Keys National Marine Sanctuary protects waters surrounding the Florida Keys. This area is home to the third-largest barrier reef in the world, as well as to over 6,000 species of marine life. Along the Highway, you will encounter many attractions to explore the Sanctuary, from swimming and diving to snorkelling and fishing. The Sanctuary is also home to a number of shipwrecks and other archaeological treasures, so it will appeal to those of you with a passion for the past. An important thing to remember is that you should wear reef-safe sunscreen if you intend to go into the water, and follow the rules and regulations in place to protect the reef.

> *If you hope to relax at white sandy beaches, this is the place to do it*

As you head down into the Lower Keys, visit the National Key Deer Refuge, which is located on Big Pine Key. This remarkable refuge protects over 8,000 acres of land on the Big Pine and No Name Keys, where the endangered Key Deer live, and is the perfect stop for any wildlife lover.

Finally, you will reach Key West, where there are countless excursions for you to enjoy, such as the Butterfly and Nature Conservatory. If you are a fan of Ernest Hemingway or American literature in general, visit the Hemingway Home, the place where the author lived during the 1930s and which is now a museum. Of course, a trip to Key West would not be complete without a walk down Duval Street, where there are endless bars, restaurants and shops to discover.

The BUILDING of CORAL CASTLE

Built to mend a broken heart, does Florida's Coral Castle contain mystical secrets that have yet to be decoded?

WORDS
Catherine Curzon

The monuments and structures of Coral Castle were built by one man, without help or machinery. He never revealed the secrets of his methods

Coral Castle, Florida

When 26-year-old Edward Leedskalnin arrived in the USA from his native Latvia just before World War I, his future looked bleak. He had been rejected by his fiancée and was suffering from tuberculosis, then a terminal disease, and he believed that his days were numbered.

Leedskalnin travelled to Florida, where he began work on a castle. He deliberately chose a remote area to ensure his privacy but, when civilisation began to move closer, he purchased a new parcel of land and began the laborious process of moving his original structures and continuing his work on what became Coral Castle. For nearly 30 years, Leedskalnin worked on in solitude, refusing to allow anyone to watch him work, but allowing visitors to view the castle for a small donation.

The castle is a masterpiece of construction and is actually made out of oolite, a sedimentary rock. Remarkably, the stones are held together without any bonding agent. It is their weight and precision placement that keeps Coral Castle standing.

As Coral Castle grew, visitors became ever more desperate to learn how one slightly-built man had achieved such a feat without any heavy machinery or assistance. Leedskalnin told them simply that it was easy when one knew how, or even teased that he had learned the secrets of the pyramid builders. He refused to give anything else away other than the tantalising suggestion that he employed perpetual motion. As interest grew, legends began to spring up around the eccentric builder, including one that he was able to move the enormous blocks of coral as though they were weightless.

Leedskalnin understood the value of self-promotion and declared that the magnetic properties of the castle had cured his terminal illness. He died in 1951, but Coral Castle is a monument to his life. Visitors to the site still seek answers as to how he was able to move the vast blocks into place with such precision, and myths have sprung up including the belief that he was able to do so by means of telekinesis or even singing to the stones, whilst still other theories posit that Leedskalnin somehow harnessed the power of the Earth itself, drawing energy from ley lines that allowed him to move the blocks with ease. Yet whether it's mathematics or magnetism, Coral Castle is a tantalising mystery waiting to be solved. Perhaps Leedskalnin has left behind a logic puzzle, but maybe it is a spell book; whatever the answer, the real solution to Coral Castle's mysterious construction has yet to be discovered. ★

Location
Homestead, Florida
~
Time zone
UTC-5

Left Edward Leedskalnin arrived in the USA with a broken heart and a terminal disease. He believed that building the remarkable castle cured both

Above The vast, nine-ton gate of Coral Castle opens at the touch of a fingertip. It is a masterpiece of precision engineering

Location
New York City
~
Time zone
UTC-5

Main When it comes to weird destinations, New York City has it all

Opposite right From deep beneath Times Square comes a constant, ominous hum; you just have to hear it over the din

Opposite bottom The Ford Foundation's greenhouse-like structure has made it an oasis in one of the world's busiest cities

New York
CITY OF WEIRD

In the city so nice they named it twice, you're never too far away from something weird

WORDS **Catherine Curzon**

New York

The Big Apple is a brash, dazzling, irresistible city that has drawn people in from all over the world, like moths to an enticing flame, since its first foundations were laid. Famed for its culture, history, and inhabitants, New York City has fascinated visitors and locals for centuries and will do so for centuries to come. Whether day or night, there's always something to do in New York, but you won't find some of the stranger must-sees in the standard tourist information guides. If you're looking for a walk on the weird side, step away from the obvious spots, tear yourself away from the glittering lights of Broadway and the stunning architectural marvels on every corner and embrace the world of weird that is hiding, waiting to ensnare even the most street-savvy visitor.

There really is something for everyone when it comes to chasing oddities in New York City, and Manhattan is packed with wonderfully weird experiences. If nautical strangeness and fairground fun are your bag, then pay a visit to the SeaGlass Carousel in Battery Park to get hands-on with a beautiful art installation. Leave behind the serenity of the ocean to join the clamouring crowds on Times Square and lose yourself in a mysterious manmade hum or venture deep beneath the streets to seek out a mysterious door that once led to New York's most glamorous address. If you'd prefer to escape the endless hustle and bustle of Manhattan, you might be surprised to learn that there's a tropical forest hidden in the heart of an anonymous office building. And you'd be wise not to whisper any secrets on a gallery high above Grand Central Station.

All of these fascinating destinations and more can be found in the celebrated city that never sleeps and all but one of them is free to enjoy or explore. From the hidden echoes of a lost and glittering age to interactive art and even a couple of classic New York destinations experienced from a decidedly different approach, no trip to Manhattan should be considered complete without them. For lovers of the weirder side of the world, taking a bite of the Big Apple is an absolute must.

The Times Square Hum
TIMES SQUARE

Times Square feels like the beating heart of the city that never sleeps and whether it's midnight or midday, the hub of humanity is always noisy. However, beneath the shouting voices and the blaring car horns is another sound, this one created in the name of art. It's easy to miss but, once you notice it, impossible to ignore.

Officially titled Times Square but known to most as the Times Square hum, it is a constant, ominous pulsating sound that reminds some - including its creator - of large bells and others of machines and engines. Created by Max Neuhaus in 1977, the sound rises from the subway grate at 45th and Broadway. Though the hum is a piece of art it is not marked by any signs, at the request of Neuhaus, who wished it to be found by accident.

The hum was silenced in 1992 due to ongoing maintenance issues but in 2002 it was brought back. To this day, the hum can still be heard.

The Ford Foundation Forest
320 EAST 43RD STREET

When Kevin Roche and John Dinkeloo built the Foundation's HQ in 1967, they did so with an eye to bringing the outside in. The atrium of the building was designed by landscape architect Dan Kiley and provides the Ford Foundation office workers with a lobby like no other.

In this building of steel and glass, deep within the heart of an urban sprawl, is a stunning tropical forest, home to innumerable plant species, tranquil pools and exotic foliage. It is an oasis in the city and acts as a massive greenhouse, guaranteeing sunlight to the plants within whilst gathered rainwater is used to feed them and ensure the necessary humidity is constant. It's the last word in urban jungles.

> *The Knickerbocker was the most celebrated hotel in all of Manhattan*

The Knickerbocker's Secret Entrance
TIMES SQUARE

In the bustling New York subway system deep beneath Times Square, thousands of people come and go day in, day out. Few of them even notice an unassuming door that they pass in their droves, hurrying past the ghost of what was once the centre of New York's social scene.

Hidden in plain sight at the eastern end of the platform for Track 1 on the S shuttle line that runs between Grand Central and Times Square-42nd Street is a simple door, dull and anonymous amongst the crowds and advertising hoardings. It could be the doorway to any storage space or broom cupboard, hundreds of which are scattered through the system, but it hides something far more evocative: this is the phantom of a city that once was. Above the easy-to-miss entrance is the only indication of what was once there, written on a tarnished brass sign displaying the word KNICKERBOCKER.

This was once the direct entrance from the subway to the Knickerbocker hotel, which stood on the corner of Broadway and 42nd Street. Built by John Jacob Astor in 1906, six years before he met his death on the Titanic, the Knickerbocker was the most celebrated hotel in all of Manhattan. It was the heart of Times Square high society and its Beaux-Arts guestrooms and bars rang to the laughter of high society, with guests including F Scott Fitzgerald, Roosevelt and Rockefeller.

The Knickerbocker closed its doors in 1920 and subsequent tenants in the building bricked up the door from within, using the space behind it for storage. Today the entrance remains sealed, a tantalising reminder of the city's glamourous past.

SeaGlass Carousel
BATTERY PARK

For a few dollars, you can be part of a stunning artwork that has been beguiling visitors to Battery Park since its unveiling in 2015. The SeaGlass Carousel is positioned on the southern tip of Manhattan atop on the site of the original New York Aquarium and is the brainchild of the Battery Conservatory and George Tsypin. Tsypin is an award-winning sculptor and stage and screen designer, who has worked at venues including La Scala and the Metropolitan Opera in New York and whose Broadway designs include *The Little Mermaid* and the ill-fated *Spider-Man: Turn Off the Dark*.

The Carousel invites riders to step inside a glass nautilus shell and choose one of 30 beautifully sculpted luminescent fish that will take them on a ride like no other. With no central pole, the fish on the carousel are free to swirl and spin around each other, offering the rider completely unobstructed views of an LED light display that makes them feel as though they are deep beneath the ocean. With a custom-composed soundtrack and ocean sounds filling the air, the SeaGlass Carousel is a truly unique experience.

New York

Whispering Gallery
GRAND CENTRAL STATION

You may be aware of the famous whispering gallery in the dome of St Paul's Cathedral, but New York has its very own example in one of its most noisy locations.

Next time you're running for a train in Grand Central Station, take the time to visit the domed lobby where walkways meet on the lower floor near the Oyster Bar & Restaurant and seek out the hidden whispering gallery. You'll know it by the distinctive herringbone pattern of the Gustavino tiles that decorate the space and it's a place where no secret is safe.

Thanks to the perfect acoustic construction, if you stand in one corner and whisper into the wall, it will be audible to anyone close to the wall in the opposite corner. It's a popular spot for marriage proposals, but what you choose to whisper is entirely up to you! ★

Above Thanks to its perfect acoustics, Grand Central Station's own whispering gallery is a must-visit

Opposite top Now a door to nowhere, this was once the entrance to one of Manhattan's most fashionable addresses

Opposite left Experience a beautiful undersea world and be part of the art, without getting your toes wet

DID YOU KNOW?!

GRAND CENTRAL STATION IS FULL OF SECRETS, INCLUDING A MYSTERIOUS ROOM THAT WAS LEFT OFF THE BLUEPRINTS, PRIVATE PRESIDENTIAL TRAIN TRACKS AND ONE OF THE CITY'S BEST HIDDEN BARS, THE CAMPBELL.

The Headless Horseman's Haunt

Many know Sleepy Hollow from TV and film, but the story is 200 years old and the village is as real (and macabre) as can be

WORDS **Rosie Cranie-Higgs**

Location
Sleepy Hollow, New York
~
Time zone
UTC-5

" *A German sharpshooter on horseback was decapitated and his body buried at Sleepy Hollow's church*

Sleepy Hollow

Possibly the most haunted village in America, Sleepy Hollow flings its arms open wide to the spooky. Even the old-style wooden welcome sign hints at gothic, ghostly happenings ahead, and in 1996, the village changed its name from its original North Tarrytown in honour of *The Legend of Sleepy Hollow*.

But the town's most famous son, author Washington Irving didn't come up with the first creepy local tale. Three centuries-old spirits are said to haunt Raven Rock: a lady in white who died in a snowstorm, a Native American girl who was driven to her death by a jealous lover, and a colonial girl who flung herself from the rock to escape an amorous raider. Cut to the 18th and 19th centuries, when the townspeople were quick to label people witches. In 1770, a doctor named Hulda was pronounced a witch by the minister of the Old Dutch Church, although she largely healed the sick by leaving baskets of herbs on their doorsteps.

To be fair, though, Irving left Sleepy Hollow's most well known mark. His inspiration is thought to be manifold but the most popular tale, backed up by the historical record, dates to the 1776 Revolutionary War. A German sharpshooter on horseback was decapitated by a cannonball during the Battle of White Plains, and his body was buried at Sleepy Hollow's Old Dutch Church. Legend and Irving have it that the Horseman rises at night to search for his head, and anyone who sees his mutilated spirit is instantly condemned to die.

Chilling? Absolutely, and Sleepy Hollow knows it. Every autumn, the local legend is brought to life. The Haunted Hayride and block party are a huge amount of fun, and Hulda's Night at Rockefeller State Park Preserve is an atmospheric, lantern-lit journey through the woods that's difficult to capture in print.

At any time of the year, Sleepy Hollow Cemetery is worth seeing, and Washington Irving's grave is decorated at Hallowe'en. Cemetery tours take place by lantern light, with town tales of insanity, corruption, and murder-suicide adding atmosphere to the Sleepy Hollow legend. The Old Dutch Church, the Headless Horseman's haunting ground, shouldn't be missed in its own right, being the second-oldest church in America.

The Headless Horseman Bridge is one of Sleepy Hollow's most popular spots. Although it's not the old bridge Irving wrote about, which has long since rotted away, the replica just upstream looks suitably timeworn and folkloric. A sign marks the spot where the original bridge stood. Nearby, and possibly even better, is local artist Linda Perlmutter's sculpture of Ichabod Crane fleeing the Horseman: 18 feet tall, the colour of cinnamon, and fantastic to see among the autumn leaves.

For shoppers, Bella's Boutique offers Sleepy Hollow-themed memorabilia such as Headless Horseman t-shirts, prints by local artists, and books on local folklore. Sleepy Hollow Gifts, mostly online but sometimes set up outside Sleepy Hollow Cemetery, prides itself on being "the home of all things headless", including a spooky Headless Horseman statue with a jack-o'-lantern head.

Finally, if you feel like going on an eerie, witchy hike, why not roam Rockefeller State Park Preserve – with trails such as Gory Brook and Witch's Spring, the longstanding ghost story of Spook Rock, and, of course, the hauntings of Raven Rock, who knows what you might meet on the trail? ★

NOT THE ONLY HEADLESS HORSEMAN IN TOWN...ISH

FROM SLEEPY HOLLOW TO IRELAND AND BEYOND, TALES LIKE THESE SPAN OCEANS

Another legendary headless horseman is the Irish Dullahan, a headless rider on a black horse who either holds his head high or carries it under his arm. Similar to Sleepy Hollow's Headless Horseman, encountering him means death if he stops, but he's not a ghost; rather, he's Unseelie, a wicked fae in faery lore. Sometimes he rides with the Death Coach, formed entirely of bones with grinning lanterns made of skulls, where he carries a long whip made of a corpse's spine.

STRANGE AT

DID YOU KNOW?!

THE FIRST ROADSIDE ATTRACTION IN THE USA IS BELIEVED TO BE LUCY THE ELEPHANT IN MARGATE, NEW JERSEY. BUILT IN 1881, IT'S CERTAINLY THE OLDEST SURVIVING. A WHOPPING SIX STOREYS TALL, SHE WAS BUILT TO ENCOURAGE PROSPECTIVE BUYERS TO STOP AND LOOK AT LAND HOLDINGS THAT WERE FOR SALE. SHE'S STILL STANDING TODAY.

TRACTIONS

Strange Attractions

The United States is home to many of the world's weirdest locations

WORDS **Ben Gazur**

For Europeans it can be hard to grasp just how large a nation the United States is. Many states within the US are larger than European countries and driving across them is quite the endevour. Long stretches of road can reveal hundreds of miles of mostly empty land. To attract those using these roads many locations developed roadside attractions to lure travellers to stop and visit (and spend money). As a result the United States has a bewildering number of attractions both weird and wonderful dotting the country.

The roadside attraction is a typically American phenomenon that grew out of the entrepreneurial spirit of the nation. Strange sites can be used as advertising locations and tourist traps to bring in money. Having a local landmarks was also a way of creating a sense of pride for those who lived in the area. Before the creation of interstate highways the network of smaller roads drivers used gave many opportunities for roadside attractions to thrive. With fewer vehicles travelling the back roads today only the most attention-grabbing locations have survived – and many of them are drawing larger numbers than ever.

Some of these strange attractions were the work of individuals who simply desired to create something. Bishop Castle was the passion project of one man to create a cottage which evolved into an eccentric castle complete with towers and arched windows. Never designed for visitors it has none the less become a roadside attraction. In the 1920s Elis Stenman constructed a summer home entirely from newspapers which had been glued together and varnished. Eventually he added a desk, piano, and clock also made from newspapers. Such was the desire to look inside that the home that it became a museum.

Other sites were built specifically to draw in the public. Many roadside sites are prefaced with boastful announcements about them containing 'The World's Largest…' These grand objects range from the world's largest ball of twine in Cawker City, Kansas, to 'The Big Duck' of Flanders, New York. The US also lays claim to gigantic forks, hammers, and pistachios to tempt tourists. As well as the man-made objects and attractions there are natural wonders which have been given mythical or historical significance. Across America a visitor can find just about any bizarre place they might imagine. Here are some of the strange sites the United States has to offer.

The World's Largest Pistachio is just one of the weird wonders America has to offer

The House on the Rock
SPRING GREEN, WISCONSIN
UTC-6

The House on the Rock was supposedly built out of spite. According to legend its design came about when Alex Jordan met with the famous architect Frank Lloyd Wright in the early 20th century. When Jordan showed the older man his plans Lloyd Wright dismissed them as childish. While driving home Jordan saw a rocky outcrop and declared he would build his fantasy there. There are historical problems with this tale but the resulting building is certainly strange enough to have born in this way.

The original house was an unusual confection of styles and soon people started visiting the house to see it – and Jordan started charging them a small fee. Since then a variety of other sights have been added. These include a display called the Heritage of the Sea featuring a vast model of a toothed whale threatening to bite guests, and the world's largest carousel. The Red Room contains an orchestra of strange instruments in a baroque hall swathed in scarlet fabric. Hanging over 60m out from the edge of the outcrop the house stands on, without any support beneath, is the Infinity Room lined with thousands of tiny windows giving expansive views of the surrounding area.

Skunk Ape Research Headquarters
OCHOPEE, FLORIDA
UTC-5

According to some the southern states of the USA are home to a large and foul-smelling creature known as the Skunk Ape. Those who have encountered it describe it in terms similar to Bigfoot - it is a tall and hairy ape or man-like beast which walks on two feet. It is said that it will occasionally stalk those walking through the wilderness or raid food supplies when it is able. Bizarre tracks left by the Skunk Ape have been observed and casts made of them, but no conclusive truth of its existence has been found.

Dave Shealy has spent many years attempting to prove that the Skunk Ape is more than a legend by searching for it in the Florida Everglades. To better educate the public he created the Skunk Ape Research Headquarters where visitors can learn about the history, habitat, and lifestyles of the Skunk Apes. According to Shealy there is a breeding population of around ten Skunk Apes living in the Everglades at any one time. To ascertain what they eat he has collected dung samples which reveal Skunk Apes will consume almost anything.

The Skunk Ape Research Headquarters contains large models of what the creatures look like and visitors can see plaster casts of their four-toed footprints. There is also a camp ground for those who wish to sleep near to the Skunk Ape's habitat. It has been voted the second best roadside attraction in the USA.

Museum of the Weird
AUSTIN, TEXAS
UTC-6

Dime museums, which displayed strange objects and human oddities for a low entrance fee were hugely popular in the 19th century. One of the few operating today can be found behind the Lucky Lizard store, which sells curiosities in Austin. The Museum of the Weird contains waxworks of legendary figures like vampires but also models of real people like John Merrick, the 'Elephant Man'. There is an example of a Feejee mermaid, which were once said to be genuine mermaids but were actually made through clever taxidermy from fish and monkeys. Visitors will also be able to see the preserved remains of a two-headed chicken and a piglet born with a single eye on its forehead.

The prize possession of the museum is the Minnesota Iceman. In the 1960s a block of ice was toured around America which was said to contain the body of a primitive human or ape-man which had been discovered in Siberia. Study suggests it is simply a rubber model but people still come from far and wide to view it.

Top left The House on the Rock contains many strange objects in its eccentrically designed rooms

Above left The Skunk Ape Research Headquarters packs a surprising variety of cryptozoological objects into its small site

Above A Feejee Mermaid, like this one, is one of the many bizarre objects collected in the Museum of the Weird

TIP
TAKE THE SKYTRAIL GONDOLA RIDE THROUGH THE REDWOODS AT THE TREES OF MYSTERY.

Strange Attractions

Left The Mütter Museum displays a range of human anatomical samples including a collection of skulls which helped disprove the pseudoscience of phrenology.

Bottom Trees of Mystery park contains both marvels of the natural world and statues of more legendary figures

Mütter Museum
PHILADELPHIA, PENNSYLVANIA
UTC-4

The Mütter Museum was founded in 1858 using a financial gift from Dr Thomas Mütter to create a collection of medical objects for the education of doctors. Mütter earned scientific fame for his work on early plastic surgery to treat those with burns and other issues with their appearance caused by illnesses. Over the years the museum has collected over 37,000 specimens and members of the museum travelled the world purchasing any items they thought might be of interest. These included anatomical models, medical instruments, and biological samples ranging from microscope slides to entire skeletons.

Today the museum is open to the public who can see many of the strange objects collected. In the Chevalier Jackson Collection of Swallowed Objects visitors can view the over 2000 items which a doctor gathered in his career. Each of them was pulled from a patient's throat and often the only payment the doctor took was to be allowed to keep them. These range from safety pins to toy dogs.

Perhaps the most gruesome displays in the Mütter Museum are those containing the remains of dead people. The skeleton of Harry Raymond Eastlack, Jr shows the dramatic changes caused by fibrodysplasia ossificans progressiva – a disease where the body replaces soft tissues with bone. Another body is known as the 'Soap Lady' because her corpse had been naturally turned into a waxy substance following her burial.

Some of the displays show only preserved parts of people. Among the collection are jars containing tattooed skin which was taken from dead people. The most famous objects in the museum are portions of Albert Einstein's brain taken by a pathologist who wanted to study it to understand his genius. Not all the objects were collected from the dead. A diseased heart in the museum was once visited by its former owner after he received a heart transplant.

Trees of Mystery
KLAMATH, CALIFORNIA
UTC-8

Trees of Mystery is a park in California which is home, as its name suggests, to several unusual Giant Redwood trees. Several trails weave through the forest to show off its many sights.

Visitors can see the Candelabra Tree with branches extending out and what look like smaller trees growing from them. There is the Elephant Tree that has a large and protuberant root system. The Cathedral Tree is actually a formation of nine trees which have grown around the rotted remains of an earlier tree. One of the largest living things in the world is the Brotherhood Tree which is nearly 300 feet tall and around 2000 years old. Those who want to get closer to the trees can walk along raised walkways strung between the trunks or travel on suspended gondolas through the canopy.

As well as the trees the park is home to a collection of huge statues called the Trail of Tall Tales that show the legend of Paul Bunyan, a giant lumberjack, and his blue ox called Babe.

House of Eternal Return
SANTA FE, NEW MEXICO
UTC-7

Large vacant spaces can blight a town if they are allowed to simply moulder, but what to do with them can be tricky to decide. In 2015 George R R Martin, author of the *Song of Ice and Fire* novels, gave over $2 million to finance the purchase of an empty bowling alley as the permanent home for a collective of artists called Meow Wolf. The 135 artists set about creating an immersive experience they titled the House of Eternal Return.

Visitors to the House of Eternal Return experience a unique trip through a bizarre two-storey home with 70 rooms purportedly containing the belongings of the Selig family. Something strange happened to them and it is left to us to try and piece together what exactly in going on in the house. There are hints to an 'Anomaly' and a group of 'Shadow Beings' called the Charter. Whole online communities have been formed attempting to bring all the information together. But the casual visitor will experience quite the trip through the Selig home.

Opening a washing machine will reveal a slide lit by strange lights the you can ride down into a room filled with lost socks. A fridge filled with glowing lights leads to another room. A cave dripping with stalactites is dominated by the luminescent skeleton of a mammoth. If you have ever wished to visit a ranch where the power is provided by hamsters running on wheels, the House of Eternal Return is one of the few places you can see such a thing.

Pike's Peak Summit House
EL PASO COUNTY, COLORADO
UTC-7

Pike's Peak stands at an altitude of 14,000 feet and was once a major landmark for travellers. When gold was discovered nearby the slogan of those setting out to strike it rich was "Pike's Peak or Bust!". While many struggled across a continent to reach Pike's Peak, and few people ever reached the top, today visitors can either drive their car up along a road or use a railway constructed for holiday makers.

At the top of the mountain travellers would find the Summit House where they could purchase a memento of their journey - and some of the most unique doughnuts anywhere on Earth. Because of the reduced air pressure at the summit, oil boils at a lower temperature, which would not be enough to cook a doughnut normally. So chefs created a special recipe to allow them to make doughnuts.

When a new visitor centre was built to replace the existing Summit House it was decided that the doughnuts had to remain. The new doughnut frying machine weighed over 1000 pounds and had to be installed before the visitor centre was constructed because it would not fit through the planned doors.

Bird Calls Phone
TAKOMA PARK, MARYLAND
UTC-5

If you lift the receiver on the public phone set up by David Schulman you may not get the call you were expecting. Instead of a person on the other end you will hear bird calls and tweets.

Created as an art project called BIRDCALLS! the phone booth provides visitors with both the sounds of various bird species and facts about them. All you have to do is pick up the handset and select a number. Pressing 1 will let you hear the songs of the mockingbird, who often mimic other birds. Number 5 provides the sounds of a rooster to honour the local Roscoe the Rooster who became a local celebrity while living wild nearby in the 1990s.

Strange Attractions

Left The House of Eternal Return contains such fantastical sights as a garden filled with glowing mushrooms

Left middle The original Summit House on Pike's Peak, where its famous donuts were first made, has been replaced with a modern visitor centre

Left below The Takoma Park phone booth, not shown, looks like any other phone booth but plays bird songs

Top right The Fountain of Youth in St Augustine is fed by water from the aquifer deep under Florida and is said to contain many health-producing minerals

Below Corona Park in Flushing Meadows was once home to a World's Fair but now hosts a zoo of retired playground animals

Fountain of Youth
ST AUGUSTINE, FLORIDA
UTC-5

Juan Ponce de León was a Spanish conquistador who led the first European expedition to Florida in 1513. While he was in search of new lands to govern a legend arose that he was actually looking for the Fountain of Youth. In 1904 the eccentric doctor Luella Day McConnell, known as 'Diamond Lil', bought land with an old well on it and declared it to be the site where Ponce de León landed. Visitors were attracted by the tall tales of Diamond Lil and the archaeological evidence discovered there which she said proved them. Today the Fountain of Youth site contains exhibits exploring the early colonial history of Florida and the Timucua people who were displaced by Europeans. Visitors can still let the waters of the spring run over their hands, drink it, and judge whether they feel rejuvenated.

> " A legend arose that he was actually looking for the Fountain of Youth

Home for Retired Playground Animals
QUEENS, NEW YORK
UTC-5

What is to be done with a working animal when it is no longer needed? In the case of concrete animals that had been placed in children's parks they have been provided a new home in New York's Flushing Meadows-Corona park. In 1964 the park hosted a World's Fair, and many of the structures used there are still standing.

The Home for Retired Playground Animals was created in 2022 to house the models of animals which designers had been mandated to include in every New York city park. When the animals were no longer required in their original parks it was decided to move them to a new home where they could be enjoyed for years to come.

The Home for Retired Playground Animals houses an aardvark, a frog, an elephant, a camel, and two dolphins all crafted from concrete. Originally they were painted but over the years much of it has washed off. When the animals were installed at the site the city held a retirement party to welcome them to their new home.

DID YOU KNOW?!

THE FIRST PLAYGROUND IN THE US OPENED IN GOLDEN GATE PARK, SAN FRANCISCO, IN 1887. VIEWED AS A STRANGE ENGLISH IDEA AT FIRST, BY 1907 THEY BECAME POPULAR.

Sliding Rock
PISGAH FOREST, NORTH CAROLINA
UTC-5

In the Pisgah Forest of North Carolina there is 60 foot long sloping layer of rock over which pour thousands of litres per minute. This flow of water and the angle of the smooth rock have turned the site into the perfect natural water slide for visitors.

No one can say when it was first discovered but the waterfall has become a popular visitor attraction in recent years. People seat themselves at the top of Sliding Rock and then enjoy the brief ride down into the natural plunge pool at the bottom. Thankfully there are handrails to help people climb back up to the top for those who want to ride down again. There is often a lifeguard present to ensure swimmers remain safe.

TIP LIFEGUARDS ARE ON DUTY AT SLIDING ROCK FROM 10AM-6PM BETWEEN MEMORIAL DAY WEEKEND AND LABOR DAY.

Above Sliding Rock has become a popular attraction for visitors looking to enjoy a natural water slide, even if the water is a little chilly

Below The Sul Ross desk looks down from the heights of Hancock Hill and visitors are invited to sit on it

Sul Ross Desk
ALPINE, TEXAS

Time zone **UTC-6**

It was around 1980 when three students at Sul Ross University called Jim Kitchen, Bill Wagner, and Travis Miller decided that they needed a new place to study that had a better view than their library and fewer noisy students. So they hauled a heavy metal desk to the top of nearby Hancock Hill, which stands around 1500m tall.

Since then the desk has become a major landmark in the area and attracts hikers who want to enjoy the scenery. In the drawer of the desk there is a notebook where visitors are invited to leave a note about themselves and others can reply. Over the decades many notebooks have been filled up and are now kept in an archive.

Strange Attractions

Above The obelisk marking the geographic centre of North America has been moved from its original site

Right The American Oddities Museum tells the story of Robert Wadlow, the world's tallest ever man, and many others

Above A Tesla coil in Griffith Observatory shows how it is possible to transfer electrical power through the air

Bottom The Echo Park Time Travel Mart operates under the slogan "Whenever you are, we're already then"

Geographical Centre of North America
RUGBY, NORTH DAKOTA
UTC-6

There was little to distinguish the town Rugby, North Dakota until in 1931 the US Geological Survey announced that it was the exact geographical centre of North America. The town immediately acted to capitalise on its new found centrality and celebrity. Locals built a 15 foot tall monument from rocks and labelled it as the centre of North America to encourage visitors. Since it was erected the obelisk has been moved to bring it closer to a major road. The town's seal was also changed to an image of North America with Rugby picked out with a red mark.

Unfortunately calculating the exact centre of a landmass is a tricky affair and several places up to a hundred miles away have also claimed to be the centre of North America. Whether Rugby is the centre or not, visitors can buy postcards to record their trip.

American Oddities Museum
ALTON, ILLINOIS
UTC-6

The American Oddities Museum began as a collection of objects related to the grim history of torture devices but has since been expanded to incorporate almost any weird and wonderful object as well.

Now the museum tells the ghost stories of Alton and the histories of some of the town's residents like Robert Wadlow, who stood nearly 9 feet tall. One of his suits is on display. Visitors are greeted by antique posters for circuses and freak shows. Inside there is a particularly grotesque Feejee mermaid and a human skeleton used by an elite society to induct its members.

The museum also tells the stories of some of the people who spent their lives in freak shows in the early 20th century through photos and records.

Griffith Observatory Tesla Coil
LOS ANGELES, CALIFORNIA
UTC-8

Griffith Observatory sits above Los Angeles and houses a planetarium and exhibits to educate the public. Inside the observatory there is a caged area that houses a large Tesla coil that dazzles people by shooting out tendrils of glowing plasma.

A Tesla coil builds up high voltages on a metal dome. Although air is a poor conductor of electricity, once enough charge is present it can leap from the coil through the surrounding air to create bolts of lightning. Several times per day the Griffith Observatory Tesla coil is activated during presentations where streams of electricity can be seen flowing from the coil to the cage around it. When it is active the electricity transferred through the air turns on a neon sign.

Echo Park Time Travel Mart
LOS ANGELES, CALIFORNIA
UTC-8

Time travellers who find themselves stuck in the wrong time are encouraged to visit the Echo Park Time Travel Mart. This shop specialises in selling items from the deep past and the far future.

Shoppers can find everything from candles scented like the Roman Forum to posters with images from the world of tomorrow. The hungry can pick up a can labelled 'Mammoth chunks'. Unfortunately the drink machine is out of order and customers are encouraged to come back yesterday.

The Echo Park Time Travel Mart is run by a non-profit organisation and all profits are used to support children with creative writing training. The texts written by students can also be bought in the shop. ★

Location
Sweetwater, Tennessee
~
Time zone
UTC-5

The Lost Sea

Descend into a network of winding caverns below Tennessee to find the largest known underground lake in the USA

WORDS Jack Griffiths

TIP YOU NEED TO PHONE THE LOST SEA ADVENTURE TO BOOK TICKETS IN ADVANCE.

Deep below the ground under East Tennessee lies a complex cave system that leads to the country's largest underground lake. Known as the Lost Sea, this 1.8 hectare (4.5 acre) lake is 42 metres (140 feet) below the foothills of the Smoky Mountains and part of the Craighead Caverns system.

The subterranean network boasts a rich history with 2000 year old tracks of a giant jaguar that is believed to have lost its way and wandered into the cave. Its bones are now in New York's American Museum of Natural History. Millennia since, the caves were used as a shelter and council by Cherokee and again by white settlers to store food, the cool cavern an ideal setting to keep vegetables fresh. Later, Confederate soldiers used the cave's resources for gunpowder during the Civil War, and were discovered by a Union spy who almost managed to destroy the setup before he was caught. Graffiti carbon-dated to 1863 proves the soldiers' presence, and alcohol was stored here during the Prohibition era, ready to be distributed for illegal drinking. The Lost Sea gets its name from the fact that it only returned to attention in 1905 when teenager Ben Sands crawled through a tiny tunnel and found the underground lake while playing in the caves. The tunnel has since been expanded considerably, first as a nightclub and social area and then as a tourist attraction. The caves and lake now host around 2000 visitors a day, keen to discover its secrets.

Visitors descend a narrow tunnel into a 120 hectare (304 acre) cave network with crystals, limestone walls, stalagmites, stalactites and a waterfall as well as historical artefacts like jewellery, arrowheads and pottery. Particularly notable are the many anthodites - rare, spiky crystals. These needle-like clusters are only found in a handful of caves around the world. Once you reach the lake, you can board a glass-bottomed electric boat to see rainbow trout swimming in the clear water. It's still unknown how many other caverns and lakes could yet be discovered in this subterranean labyrinth. More than 5.2 hectares (13 acres) of water have been mapped out so far but there could be more with many areas still completely submerged. It may be the largest known underground lake in the USA but it is the second largest in the world (that's not beneath a glacier) after Namibia's Dragon's Breath Cave. ★

Top right The Lost Sea Adventure is a thriving visitor attraction where you can experience the wonder and majesty of these water-filled caverns for yourself

Right The entrance to the Lost Sea, also known as Craighead Caverns, listed as a National Natural Landmark by the National Park Service in 1973

Far right Some of the spectacular anthodite crystal formations inside the caverns

The Lost Sea

"Ben Sands crawled through a tiny tunnel and found the lake"

DID YOU KNOW?!

THE ORIGINAL NAME FOR THE CAVES, CRAIGHEAD CAVERNS, COMES FROM THE NAME OF THE CHIEF OF THE CHEROKEE WHO USED TO MEET THERE. THEY WERE REFERRED TO BY THIS NAME UNTIL THE LAKE WAS DISCOVERED IN 1905.

Main Explore the peculiarities of California's Golden City

Opposite right Come for the 163 steps of art, stay for the lush greenery and sweeping views

Opposite bottom San Fran had more than 800 saloons in 1870 but Burnell saw the opportunity for something a bit different

Location
San Francisco, California
~
Time zone
UTC-8

Strange SAN FRANCISCO

From the ocean's very own instrument to indoor mazes, San Francisco is varied in its weirdness

WORDS **Jack Griffiths**

San Francisco is instantly recognisable for the Golden Gate Bridge and its famous cable cars that transport people around the notoriously hilly city with more than 50 hills. Also known as the Golden City, San Francisco had just acquired its name when the California Gold Rush attracted a population boom, increasing its number of residents from 1,000 in 1848 to 25,000 in 1849.

The city continued to grow rapidly into the early 20th century, but its rise was curtailed by the earthquake of 1906 when fires engulfed the city, caused by ruptured gas and power lines. Around 700 people died and 80 per cent of the city was destroyed, encouraging the city to invest in concrete buildings rather than wooden structures, but lots of damage was still sustained in another quake that hit in 1989. Since then, efforts have been made to partially shake-proof buildings from seismic activity, including a retrofit of San Francisco International Airport that cost billions of dollars.

Nevertheless, tens of millions of people visit San Francisco every year. The city is famous for its misty fog that descends in the summer, blocking the sun and causing a drop in temperature. The mist has led to San Francisco being dubbed 'Fog City', one of its many nicknames, and is caused by warm air meeting cold water. San Fran is also big into its beer. The city had 800 saloons and 24 breweries by 1860 and, a decade later, it even had a brewery operating out of a castle.

Being such a hilly city means there are a lot of steps. Some are well worth the climb though, and not just for the view at the top. The 16th Avenue Tiled Steps are decorated with beautiful mosaics that take walkers on a journey while the infamous Lincoln Park steps are a marvel in themselves.

So what exactly is weird about this magnificent city then? Well, you can hear what the sea would sound like if it could play an instrument, for one thing. Fancy getting lost in an indoor maze while your senses are barraged by sound and confused by vision? You can do that too. If a psychedelic labyrinth isn't up your street, why not take a nostaligic, adrenaline-fueled trip down a community-made slide in the heart of the Noe Valley neighbourhood? You never know, Frisco might just become your favourite weird city.

Secret Tiled Staircase
GOLDEN GATE HEIGHTS

San Francisco is a hilly place so it comes as no surprise that there are more than 600 public staircases in the city. Not many are as bright and beautiful as the 16th Avenue Tiled Steps, a staircase adorned with marvellous mosaics up and down them.

The artwork, made with more than 2,000 unique tiles and 75,000 glass fragments, is meant to represent everything from the sea to the stars, starting with swimming fish and finishing with soaring birds. It's inspired by the just as wondrous Selarón staircase in Rio de Janeiro and all the designs are community-donated.

The staircase's popularity has helped revitalise the local area and some people even sponsor some of the steps. Once you've finished looking down at the colours, look up and you'll be able to view San Fran's Sunset District and the Pacific Ocean.

Albion Castle
INDIA BASIN

This brewery within a castle has a rich history. Built in 1870 by English brewer John Hamlyn Burnell, it supplied the growing city with beer and ale, just like back in the Old World. Its underground spring provides up to 10,000 gallons of fresh water every day -perfect for brewing.

During Prohibition, the brewery was closed and instead provided the area with refreshing drinking water. The castle was almost demolished in 1961 but was saved from the bulldozers due to its importance as a source of clean water - in case of a potential nuclear attack. Since 1998, it has been used for events and functions but remains an intriguing oddity, a castle modelled on Norman fortifications in San Francisco.

> *“ Blacklights emit ultraviolet light and disorientate everyone as they enter*

The Wave Organ
MARINA DISTRICT

Hear the true sounds of the sea with the Wave Organ at San Francisco Bay. This musical instrument amplifies music created by the crash of waves. A granite and marble sculpture on a jetty in the bay, it is inspired by sounds from underground pipes in Sydney, Australia.

As the water enters and then leaves the 20-plus pipes, it creates different sounds. The more water, the lower the sound and vice versa. The timbre of the tune changes depending on the strength of the waves and ranges from quiet sloshes to loud rumbles, reminiscent of distant humming or deep breathing. It was completed in 1986 and sits on a jetty made of material from an old cemetery while the organ itself is a mix of concrete and PVC.

The organ was the brainchild of Frank Oppenheimer, the brother of the 'father of the atomic bomb', J Robert Oppenheimer. The first prototype was unveiled in 1981 but it took a while for support, grants and fundraising to gather pace. Sadly, Frank died the year before it was finished and the organ is dedicated to his memory. Work on the organ was completed by artists Peter Richards and sculptor George Gonzales from the city's Exploratorium museum.

It's a tranquil place to hear the ocean play its very own musical instrument and there are benches nearby where you can sit, relax and listen to the odd hisses and splashes created by the waves. You can stimulate your sense of sight too with a panorama of Alcatraz, Downtown San Francisco and the Golden Gate Bridge.

Magowan's Infinite Mirror Maze
PIER 39

San Fran's Pier 39 has a number of attractions including seals, carnival rides and escape rooms. Since 2009, visitors have been encouraged to 'Get lost in the Infinite' at Magowan's Infinite Mirror Maze.

In reality, there aren't quite an infinite amount of mirrors (in fact, there's 77) but it certainly seems like it. Blacklights emit ultraviolet light and disorientate everyone as they enter. The aim of the game is to escape the maze but this is easier said than done as the labyrinth's psychedelic experience assaults your senses and makes you question what is and what isn't real.

The maze's creator Charles Magowan based it on the psychedelic scene of the 1960s and '70s and old carnival fun houses. Getting out of the 2000 square foot maze isn't easy, with dead ends and perplexing mirrors that distort realityas well as neon lights and loud music. Some say that feeling your way round is the best way. Others say that you've not done it right until you've completed it backwards.

DID YOU KNOW?!

14-YEAR-OLD KIM CLARK DESIGNED THE ICONIC CONCRETE SLIDES FOUND IN SEWARD MINI PARK AFTER WINNING A COMPETITION RUN BY SCULPTOR RUTH ASAWA. THE SLIDES ARE OPEN TUESDAY THROUGH SUNDAY FROM 10AM TO 6PM.

Seward Street Slides
SEWARD MINI PARK

Since 1973, a small neighbourhood in Seward Mini Park has been enjoying a simple pleasure, thanks to community activism. These steep two-storey 40-feet long dual concrete slides offer great views of the city centre from the top, followed by a quick descent down. Frequent flyers on the Noe Valley neighbourhood slides recommend using a piece of cardboard to increase your speed, but also advise you to wear hardy trousers.

The slides are next to a community garden and saw the light of the day after a teenager Kim Clark won a competition to decide how to improve the neighbourhood. They were designed both as fun for children and nostalgia for adults and were created after community resistance to a new housing project.

One of the slides is slightly steeper and quicker than the other so thrill-seekers should choose this one. Sliders end up in a pool of sand at the bottom and, if you want to go even faster, sprinkling sand on the slide itself is meant to increase your top speed. ★

Above Re-live your childhood at Seward Street Slides

Opposite top The Wave Organ's been in place since 1986 and, naturally, the best time to see it is at high tide

Opposite left Visitors to Magowan's Infinite Mirror Maze are required to wear plastic gloves so they don't smear the mirrors

The Bridgewater Triangle

This area of southeastern Massachusetts is reputedly a paranormal powerhouse

WORDS Alice Pattillo

Location Massachusetts ~ **Time zone** UTC-5

The land equivalent of the infamous Bermuda Triangle, the Bridgewater Triangle is a 200 square mile area of Southeastern Massachusetts between Abington, Freetown and Rehoboth. It's a magnet for paranormal activity ranging from UFOs and supernatural humanoids to non-native animal sightings and abnormally large, vicious hounds. The land is reputed to be cursed due to a revered object, the wampum belt, being lost during King Philip's War (1675-1678), the conflict between the colonists and their indigenous allies, the Wampanoag. The Wampanoag told tales of folkloric creatures named pukwudgies who made the area their home. These porcupine-backed goblins often lure humans into forests to meet an unfortunate end. You might spot one in Freetown-Fall River State Forest - the site of numerous murders, reported Satanic cult activity (including animal sacrifice) and misfortunes - or near Lake Nippenicket in Hockomock Swamp (Wampanoag for "where spirits dwell"). Colonial settlers dubbed this vegetated freshwater wetland "Devil's Swamp". At the very centre of the paranormal vortex, it's rife with supernatural activity from phantom fires and "spook lights" to roaming spectres, indigenous cryptids like Thunderbirds (gigantic pterodactyl-like birds) and even Bigfoot.

Murderer Lizzie Borden's house is located within the Bridgewater Triangle, as is Taunton State Hospital, a psychiatric institution that performed many questionable experiments on patients and supposedly conducted Satanic rituals in the basement, where strange markings can still be seen. The hospital also treated at least two murderers - Anthony Santo, who killed two of his cousins and a six-year-old girl, and Honora "Jolly Jane" Toppan, a psychotic nurse and prolific serial killer, who admitted to getting an erotic thrill from holding her victims while they died. Unsurprisingly, the hospital is a hotbed of paranormal activity.

In Rehoboth, the historic one-room schoolhouse, Hornbine School, built in 1862, now functions as a museum, but it also has its fair share of ghostly activity, and local highway Route 44 is haunted by a red-headed, flannel-clad hitchhiker. Over in Bridgewater itself, Bridgewater State University is also rumoured to be riddled with ghosts, in particular Woodward Hall. ★

Bridgewater Triangle

> It's a magnet for paranormal activity ranging from UFOs to supernatural humanoids

Main Is the lake home to dark spirits?

Right Bridgewater State University is haunted

Below A mystical Native artefact was lost

Bottom right The triangle between Abington, Rehoboth and Freetown

DID YOU KNOW?!

THE NAME "BRIDGEWATER TRIANGLE" WAS COINED BY THE FAMOUS CRYPTOZOOLOGIST LOREN COLEMAN. A CRYPTOZOOLOGIST IS SOMEONE WHO FOCUSES ON SEARCHING FOR LEGENDARY OR URBAN-MYTHICAL CREATURES THAT AREN'T OFFICIALLY KNOWN TO REGULAR SCIENCE, LIKE NESSIE OR BIGFOOT.

Covering thirteen states from southern New York to northern Mississippi, Appalachia includes dark forests and a 480-million-year-old mountain range that is said to be home to some of the world's strangest supernatural entities and freakiest legends. The geography of this ancient, sprawling landscape shifts from lush, green valleys to jutting crags and steep, rocky cliffs, criss-crossed by a vast network of rivers. Thriving cities, such as Pittsburg and Knoxville, offer a different aspect of Appalachia, but even their bustling towns can't escape its supernatural reputation.

The reason for such a high percentage of uncanny tales across the 206,000 square miles can, to a large extent, be explained by Appalachia's fascinating cultural melting pot. Long before European settlers arrived, the

Locations
Georgia, Kentucky, North Carolina, Tennessee, West Virginia
~
Time zone
Various

EERIE

Looking for the bizarre and unusual?

Appalachia is your one-stop-shop for all things weird

Who knows what uncanny entities hide within the misty Appalachian Mountains

The Appalachians

Appalachian region was inhabited by a number of Native American tribes including the Cherokee, Powhatan, Shawnee, Saponi and Monacan. Each group passed down their legends and cosmology, using stories to explain their surrounding landscape. Cherokee lore, for example, tells of a giant buzzard that plummeted to the ground, flapped his wings and in doing so, created the Great Smoky Mountains. As with European folklore, Native American lore was used to warn children of the dangers of forests after dark. Shapeshifting entities such as Spearfinger, a stone-skinned witch with a knife for one of her fingers, is still whispered to lurk in the shadows of the Appalachian mountains.

The Scottish and Irish settlers brought with them a wealth of Celtic mythology. Talk of banshees and fae folk blended with the Wendigo and tree spirits until the region was saturated with supernatural beliefs.

Visitors may well scoff at the local superstitions but fear of otherworldly creatures remain very much alive across rural areas. Should you pass a cemetery on your trip, the Appalachian people will advise you to hold your breath so no wandering spirit can enter your body, and if you take a rest in a rocking chair, you will be told to stop it from rocking before walking away since you might invite spirits into the home.

Holidaymakers may dismiss these stories as ancient tittle-tattle and old wives' tales but strange sightings and inexplicable events continue to happen to this day. Mysterious man-beasts and ghostly floating lights caught on camera are far harder to dismiss. From Mothman to Bigfoot, Raw Head and Bloody Bones to the Blue Ghost Fireflies, this ancient region has it all. Welcome to eerie Appalachia!

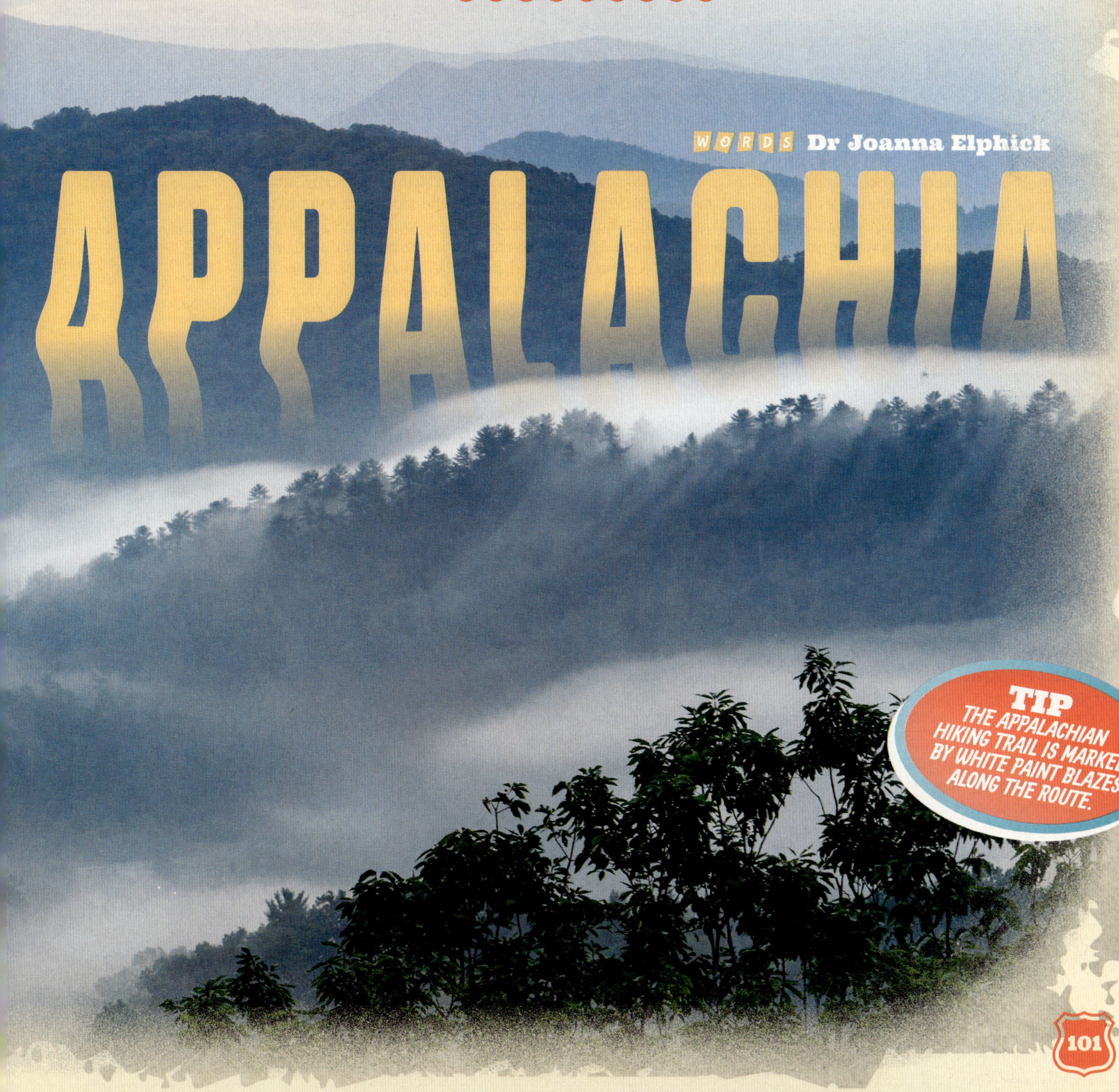

APPALACHIA

WORDS Dr Joanna Elphick

TIP THE APPALACHIAN HIKING TRAIL IS MARKED BY WHITE PAINT BLAZES ALONG THE ROUTE.

Top left President Andrew Jackson, witnessed the Bell Witch with his own eyes

Middle top The ghost of baggage master Hugh K Linster, whose body was recovered from the 1891 wreckage, is also seen waving a gold watch

Middle under Tourists wait at the scenic view point to watch the mysterious light show on Brown Mountain

Above Some believe the Moon-Eyed People were an albino tribe similar to the Zuni Tribe from New Mexio

The Bell Witch
ROBERTSON COUNTY, TENNESSEE
UTC-6

In 1818, John Bell and his well-respected family became the epicentre of one of America's most infamous hauntings. Initially, the unexplained activities were nothing more than strange banging in the middle of the night, gnawing sounds, and unidentifiable scratching down the wooden doors and walls. However, things quickly progressed and it wasn't long before the Bells' daughters were being pinched in the dark and wrenched from their beds..

John Bell tried to keep the events a secret, fearful of the reaction from the church-going community, but when a close friend witnessed furniture being dragged across the floor and objects flying of their own accord, word of the poltergeist soon got out.

Gaining strength from the attention, the entity began talking, introducing herself as the spirit of Kate Batts, a local witch. People came from far and wide to commune with 'Old Kate' and hear her recite sermons and sing hymns. When John Bell died, the entity claimed she had poisoned him and continued to torment the family until finally disappearing in 1828, having seemingly grown tired of the remaining Bell family.

The Bostian Bridge Ghost Train
WEST OF STATESVILLE, IREDELL COUNTY, NORTH CAROLINA
UTC-5

In 1891, a train derailed whilst crossing the Bostian Bridge and plummeted into the creek. Twenty-two passengers perished as the clock struck 3:00 am. Fifty years later, a woman watched in horror as a ghostly train rushed along the tracks before swerving off the bridge and disappearing into the same creek.

Word soon spread of the ghost train and people began camping on the verges, hoping for a sight of the haunted carriages. In 2010, a ghost hunter was on the bridge when he heard a train whistle. Believing it to be the ghost train he stood on the tracks to get a better view. A real train struck him, killing him instantly. It was 3:00 am precisely.

The Brown Mountain Lights
BROWN MOUNTAIN, NORTH CAROLINA
UTC-5

In 1771, an engineer wrote in his diary about a series of lights he had seen floating over Brown Mountain in North Carolina. By 1922, enough people had witnessed the glowing orbs that the United States Ecological Society were sent to investigate them. After extensive research, the society concluded they were nothing more than passing car headlights. Strange then that they had been witnessed long before the first car had been invented. The theory was literally blown out of the water after a flood took out all roads across the mountain and the eerie lights continued to glow.

The mysterious lights continue to amaze. ppalachian State University has studied the strange phenomena and determined that it is almost certainly natural gases forming, similar to will-o'-the-wisp, seen by those travelling through marshes at night but the Cherokee maintain that they are the ghost torches of heartbroken female spirits searching for their husbands after a bloody battle on Brown Mountain where none returned home.

The Moon-Eyed People
GEORGIA
UTC-5

Cherokee legend tells of a mysterious tribe of tiny people with pale skin, blond beards and luminous blue eyes who lived in a network of caves in the Appalachian mountains. Anthropologists initially believed the tribe may have been Welsh settlers but the Cherokee claim that they were there long before even the Native Americans had arrived. A three-foot-tall statue, discovered where the Hiwasse and Valley Rivers meet, pre-dates the Cherokee, supporting their oral tradition of the little people. Apparently, their saucer-like eyes were so sensitive to the light that they were forced to become a nocturnal tribe, coming out to hunt after dark. The Cherokee eventually drove the Moon-Eyed People away during a fierce -battle at Fort Mountain, leaving behind a stone wall, zigzagging across Fort Mountain State Park, supposedly built by the mysterious tribe to keep the Native Americans back.

Mothman
POINT PLEASANT, WEST VIRGINIA

Time zone **UTC-5**

Throughout 1966, a period of bizarre phenomena terrified the people of West Virginia. On 12 November, five men were digging a grave when a large shadow fell over them. Looking up into the air they were horrified to witness an enormous humanoid creature with wings soaring over their heads. They estimated that it had a ten-foot wingspan and red glowing eyes.

Two couples reported seeing a monstrous man-bird with round ruby eyes whilst driving past an old TNT factory. They drove straight to Point Pleasant Police Station, telling the sheriff that the creature had remained parallel to their car despite them travelling at over 100-miles-per-hour. Something was stalking the people of Point Pleasant and the local newspaper decided to name it 'Mothman'. Further sightings followed and it wasn't long before the legend of West Virginia's very own cryptid was born. Witnesses claimed that, following their brush with the creature, they were plagued with recurring nightmares ending in tragedy.

However, a year after the first sighting, an all too real disaster took place when the Silver Bridge collapsed during rush hour. 46 people perished as their cars tumbled into the Ohio River. Locals claimed to have seen Mothman standing on the bridge the day before the tragedy, leading to rumours that the creature was a portent of doom.

Although the sightings diminished, they haven't entirely stopped and witnesses still come forward now and again with accounts of the mysterious Mothman.

Should you visit Point Pleasant on the third weekend in September, you are guaranteed a sighting at the Mothman Festival.

TIP
THE MOTHMAN MUSEUM IN POINT PLEASANT IS OPEN SEVEN DAYS A WEEK (EXCEPT HOLIDAYS).

> *Witnesses still come forward with accounts of the mysterious Mothman*

DID YOU KNOW?!

IN THE CHEROKEE LANGUAGE, RAVEN MOCKERS ARE REFERRED TO AS "KÂ'LANÛ AHKYELI'SKÏ" ('THE DEATH SPIRIT') AND "TSUNDIGE'WI" WHICH MEANS 'HE WHO COVERS HIS FACE'.

The Raven Mocker
BLUE RIDGE MOUNTAINS, BURKE COUNTY
UTC-5

These monstrous entities are known in Cherokee lore to suck the breath from the sick and wounded. Thought to be drawn to the homes of the nearly departed, they sit upon their chest, pushing out their final gasp. They then remove and consume the heart, capturing the last heartbeat. This, the Cherokee believe, is how they prolong their own miserable lives.

The Raven Mockers disguise themselves as elderly folk in order to get close to vulnerable members of the community. Like vultures waiting for their prey to drop, the creatures bide their time waiting to steal the remaining lifeforce. The only way to repel a Raven Mocker is to witness its true form. Should a shaman catch sight of it in all its hideous glory, it will die within seven days.

They are said to fly through the night sky with their arms stretched out before them, their skeletal hands reaching out into the darkness, sparks trailing behind. As they plummet to the ground they emit a shriek like that of a cawing raven.

Kuwohi
GREAT SMOKY MOUNTAINS, BRYSON CITY, NORTH CAROLINA
UTC-5

To tourists, Kuwohi is the highest of the Great Smoky Mountains and a beautiful place for a selfie whilst on the Appalachian Trial, but to the Cherokee, it is a place of spiritual importance since it was here that the Medicine People came to commune with their Creator and ask for guidance.

The name 'Kuwohi' means 'mulberry place' in reference to the practice of the Cherokee people climbing the mountain to reach the mulberries that were used in medicine. The fact that it is the highest point within their homeland was of importance since they were closest to their Creator. Today the Cherokee take their children to the mountain top to teach them the spiritual heritage to be found here.

Top left A brave must ask the Medicine Man to identify the Raven Mocker for he is the only member of the tribe to see it in its natural form

Above left With an elevation of 6,643 feet, Kuwohi it the tallest of the Great Smoky Mountains and the highest point in Tennessee

Above Locals advise hikers to travel in pairs and to take heed of the warning signs!

The Appalachians

The Flatwoods Monster
FLATWOODS, GREENUP COUNTY, KENTUCKY
UTC-5

In 1952, four boys watched as a UFO shot across the darkening sky and crashed into the hillside. The six ran to the crash site to investigate. By now it was getting dark but the boys could pinpoint the location clearly as there was a pulsing red light where the UFO had struck. When they shone a torch, they saw a ten-foot-tall being floating towards them. The creature had glowing eyes, a spade-shaped head, taloned hands and, most strangely, was wearing a shimmering metallic dress. The investigators took off when the creature hissed and began to glide towards them. The next day there was no sign of the crash but anyone close to the site quickly became violently sick.

The Mountain Dew Headstone
OAK HILL CEMETERY, JOHNSON CITY, TENNESSEE
UTC-5

It isn't often that you visit a cemetery and find something to laugh about, but at Oak Hill you are guaranteed to leave with a smile on your face. Only in weird Appalachia will you find a headstone in honour of a Tennessee institution, Mountain Dew.

The monument, carved in the shape of a six-feet-tall bottle, is decorated with the original imagery of 'Willie the Hillbilly', carrying his rifle and a jug of moonshine. The look was later dropped by the Pepsi-Cola Company but Americans fondly remember the tagline, 'It'll tickle yore innards!', and fans travel from all over to raise a glass to their favourite soft drink. It even has a built-in bottle opener in case you forget to bring one.

Bigfoot
ADIRONDACKS, NEW YORK – BLUE RIDGE MOUNTAINS, NORTH CAROLINA
UTC-5

Surely the most famous cryptid in the world, Bigfoot has been spotted in a multitude of locations and, whilst the vast majority of sightings have occurred across Washington State, many have claimed to spot the harmless, hairy humanoid in the Appalachian region. The area is a perfect habitat for the shy and elusive bipedal ape-man, where it can hide in the cavernous cave systems, hunt in the dense, dark forests, and drink from the criss-crossing Appalachian rivers without constantly stumbling across a nosy human.

The Native American tribes of the Appalachian Mountains speak of their own hairy apemen folklore and these tales are thought to be the basis of many Bigfoot stories. The local Cherokee tell of the Tsul 'Kalu, a group of bipedal creatures described as 'slant-eyed giants' who inhabit the mountains. Other tribes refer to the mysterious 'Ghost Bears'.

Whilst many modern day accounts are dismissed as misidentified black bears standing up on their hind feet, Bigfoot sightings are regularly made, particularly along the Appalachian Trail and throughout the Monongahela National Forest in West Virginia, where accounts of territorial boulder throwing and eerie calls have been noted for decades.

Left Tourists can sit in the Flatwoods Monster Visitor Centre chair for a golden photo opportunity

Below The name 'Mountain Dew' is a colloquial term in Tennessee for moonshine, illegal homemade whiskey

Bottom Are Wampus Cat's supernatural glowing eyes nothing more than a cougar caught in the light?

The Wampus Cat
NORTH CAROLINA
UTC-5

Appalachian farmers and hunters warn their children not to stray into the forest after dark for fear of the mighty Wampus Cat. Over the centuries, it has been accused of taking livestock and terrifying hikers but sadly, there is little in the way of actual evidence of its existence. Some believe the creature is an unknown breed of wild cat whilst others state it is a supernatural six-legged being or unidentified cryptid. The Cherokee tell of a Native American woman who dressed in the pelt of a cougar to spy on the pre-hunting rituals of the tribal warriors. As the shaman was carrying out the ceremony, he caught sight of the woman and promptly transformed her into a catwoman as a punishment. The woman was furious and this, they claim, explains the violent attacks on the local wildlife.

Whether she is a rare feline, a magical hybrid or an Appalachian cryptid, Wampus Cat is regularly spotted along the Appalachian Trail and is known to cause havoc wherever she goes. ★

America's Answer to Stonehenge

CARH

Location
Alliance, Nebraska

Time zone
UTC-7

Jim Reinders, a native of Nebraska, lived for several years in London and enjoyed taking visitors to view the massive standing stones of Stonehenge. This stone circle from over 4000 years ago stands on the expanse of Salisbury Plain and Reinders was struck by the resemblance of this landscape to his home state. He began to ponder whether a similar site could be constructed there.

When Reinders' father died in 1982 he started a plan to honour him with an American version of Stonehenge. In 1987 he began to dig pits on land his father once farmed and into the holes he erected the hulks of American-made automobiles. These cars would stand upright in exactly the same pattern as the great stones of Stonehenge. When Reinders was asked why he chose to use cars instead of stone he simply said that stone was too expensive. Almost immediately locals noticed what was happening and Reinders was visited by police who found it amusing, but noted that others thought it was an eyesore. Reinders was not deterred and he sprayed the cars with grey paint to better mimic Stonehenge. In total 39 vehicles were used to create the site.

Main The Carhenge site is now home to a number of other sculptures crafted from automobiles for visitors to enjoy

Middle The grey-painted cars of Carhenge were erected to exactly follow the plan of Stonehenge, with Fords, Cadillacs, and Oldsmobiles all incorporated

Middle right Just as at the original Stonehenge, on certain days of the year the sun rises in alignment with some of the standing 'stones'

...ENGE

Carhenge, Nebraska

On the High Plains of Nebraska visitors can see a replica of an ancient monument, but made from American automobiles

WORDS Ben Gazur

At the summer solstice (which is when the rising of the sun aligns with the standing stones of Stonehenge) in 1987, the Reinders family gathered at Carhenge to honour their dead father. Champagne was drunk, poetry declaimed, and songs sung. Once Carhenge was constructed, Reinders wanted it to remain in place for a long time. Some locals however continued to view it as a blight on the landscape. One neighbour designed a house they were building so that it would not look out onto Carhenge at all.

Others treated it as an interesting landmark which deserved to be visited. In 2006 a visitor centre was built to welcome people and show the history of the site. Since it was erected other sculptures made by Reinders and other artists have been added to create a Car Art Reserve. Visitors can see a car transformed into a salmon leaping from the earth and a dinosaur skeleton made from car parts.

The whole area has been donated to the city of Alliance and is free to visit and open at all hours. Though Reinders did not know it when he started, Carhenge was built in the path of the 2017 total solar eclipse, and thousands of people came to view it from the site. ★

> " *He erected the hulks of American-made automobiles* "

Main From Hollywood to Venice Beach, there is more to Tinseltown than meets the eye

Opposite right Take a seat and chow down on a sandwich where the wild things were at Griffith Park's abandoned zoo

Opposite bottom Also known as El Alisal, Lummis house now a museum

Location
Los Angeles, California
~
Time zone
UTC-8

La La Land
LOS ANGELES

Less Hollywood Sign and Santa Monica Pier, more Chicken Boy and Sunken City

WORDS **Jack Griffiths**

Los Angeles

Los Angeles, the City of the Angels, is one of the world's megacities. The USA's second largest city is famous for its movie and music scene and is situated on a Pacific coastal basin with beaches, mountains, rivers and tectonic fault lines. It was a beacon of hope and the endpoint for many white settlers migrating west on the California Trail. It's known worldwide for Hollywood - its gigantic white letters standing proud atop Mount Lee - the Walk of Fame, the Sunset Strip, Hollywood Bowl, Dodger Stadium, Venice Beach and Santa Monica Pier. Even its concrete flood channels are a thing of legend. Away from all the glitz, glamour and well-known landmarks, it is also home to more than its fair share of weird and wonderful sites.

LA culture comprises California's indigenous history, the city's role as a Spanish frontier outpost and its modern day reputation as Tinseltown, the home of the rich and famous. Lummis Home showcases the first two, a museum and former home of a famous Renaissance Man who was captivated by the cultural heritage of the American Southwest. Meanwhile, over in Downtown, the Bradbury Building is iconic inside and out and reveals a history that the city isn't often associated with - the Victorian era. Of course, being Los Angeles, it is more commonly remembered for its presence in a number of Hollywood films.

Angelenos are aware of the possibility of earthquakes in their city, LA sitting on the notorious San Andreas Fault, a break in the Earth's crust that can result in quakes. The Sunken City may not have been caused by an earthquake, but its battered remains demonstrate the power of nature, even in such an urbanised area, and the fascination with visiting a disaster area.

Some of the weirdness is more light-hearted. Los Angeles has a number of strange statues - such as the Corporate Head and the Ballerina Clown. Both don't quite meet the levels of oddity that Chicken Boy provides, a publicity stunt turned LA institution. Talking about institutions, Griffith Park Zoo was a popular park between 1912 and its closure in 1966, drawing in more than two million visitors a year at its peak. Today, it's long gone with Los Angeles Zoo taking the mantle as the city's home for animals - but its abandoned remains have become a popular picnic spot and you can wander through the ruins of enclosures where lions, monkeys and bears once roamed.

Old Zoo Picnic Area
GRIFFITH PARK

Griffith Park is one of the largest parks in LA, containing an observatory, the famous Hollywood Sign and also, bizarrely, a place where you can picnic as if you were an animal in a zoo. Venture inside the remnants of the city's first zoo, in enclosures where bears, monkeys and elephants used to be.

This unusual opportunity came to be after the first Los Angeles Zoo closed in 1966 when it fell into financial trouble and was superseded by the city's current zoo. The zoo had a tortured history following its opening in 1912 with reports of substandard cages, sewage leaks and injured animals.

Instead of building anything new, the site was repurposed into a unique space for family picnics with benches installed so you can eat where the animals used to live. The area is either eerie or historic, depending on your outlook but, either way, it is remarkably untouched and you're able to clamber into the large enclosures, as well as venture into the smaller cages.

Lummis Home
NORTHEAST LOS ANGELES

The Lummis House is a fascinating example of late 19th century architecture. It was designed by Charles F Lummis and built purposely from a mixture of stone and wood as to fit in with its natural surroundings. Lummis, a polymath who was the first City Editor at the *LA Times* as well as a poet, athlete and historian, walked more than 3,500 miles from Cincinnati to Los Angeles. After his epic journey, he decided that he needed to build a centre to preserve the indigenous cultural heritage of the American Southwest.

Its striking rock tower, with its bulging stone face, was a retreat for intelligent discussion on heritage, with visitors including environmental philosopher John Muir, composer John Philip Sousa and social commentator Will Rogers. Inside you'll find Lummis' collections of writings, photographs and other historic artefacts.

> *"Chicken Boy still stands, bucket in hand, a testament to a bygone era"*

Sunken City
SAN PEDRO

Point Fermin was once a coastal neighbourhood on the south side of Los Angeles, boasting excellent views of the Pacific Ocean. However, in January 1929, cracks began appearing in the street, breaking streets and pipelines. As the cracks widened, residents were evacuated and the houses were purchased by the city. Thankfully, everyone was evacuated before what was left of their home slowly fell off the cliffs in a gradual landslide. Today, up on the cliff, graffiti-covered concrete fragments of pavement, house foundations and rail tracks are all that remains of the real estate, now cracked and entangled with trees and bushes. On the shoreline below, the rest of the nighbourhood is slowly eroded by the crashing waves. What was Point Fermin is now known as Sunken City.

The landslides were caused due to the California coast being an active tectonic environment that lies along the San Andreas faultline. The San Pedro cliffs are composed of clay and other soft sediments, making them more easily eroded, unstable and prone to landslides.

Construction has not been attempted since due to the dangers and the area remained relatively unknown until a boost in popularity on social media. This has attracted anti-social behaviour to the area as well as people falling from the cliffs to their deaths, including a kicker from the University of Southern California American Football team. The area is now fenced off and it is illegal to set foot in the Sunken City but it is possible to view the remains from nearby trails.

Bradbury Building
DOWNTOWN

Downtown's oldest commercial building is an iconic structure with a colourful history. Constructed in 1893, stepping inside the imposing structure is like going back in time to the Victorian era with open cage lifts and marble stairs ascending its grand atrium.

The building was initially office space and is named after mine owner turned real estate mogul, Louis Bradbury. Bradbury tasked then-rookie architect George Wyman with its construction. Overwhelmed by the responsibility, Wyman allegedly sought paranormal advice through a Ouija board to decide if he should pursue the opportunity or not. We have the architect's dead brother to thank for being able to experience the building's beauty and splendour as it was him who convinced Wyman to go ahead with the project. Not just aesthetically pleasing, the building also had advanced ventilation systems for the time, allowing for a comfortable visit as you take in in the stained glass, hand-carved woodwork and wrought-iron balconies.

Wyman was supposedly inspired by science fiction novels for the building's design and it has featured in a number of blockbuster films including the sci-fi classic *Blade Runner*.

Below Chicken Boy is 22-foot tall and stands over Route 66, in constant watch over the city

Opposite top All that's left of Point Fermin is graffitied slabs of pavement, cracked and left to decay

Opposite left Weekly walking tours of LA's historic downtown take in the Bradbury Building which still has human conductors operating its lifts

Los Angeles

Chicken Boy
HIGHLAND PARK

Sometimes known as the Statue of Liberty of Los Angeles, Chicken Boy is what it says on the tin, a giant adolescent man-chicken hybrid. This fowl oddity stands atop the roof of Future Studio Gallery and is a famous example of a Muffler Man, a large fibreglass figure often used to advertise products in the 1960s. The fried chicken restaurant that the bird once promoted is long gone but Chicken Boy still stands, bucket in hand, a testament to a bygone era.

Former governor of California, Arnold Schwarzenegger, was seemingly a fan and granted the statue a Governor's Historic Preservation Award. The bird-man even has its own film (1991's 30-minute long *Chicken Boy: The Movie*) and merch if you fancy a poultry-based t-shirt, pen or bag. ★

DID YOU KNOW?!

ORIGINALLY ERECTED ABOVE CHICKEN BOY FRIED CHICKEN LOCATED ON BROADWAY, THE RESTAURANT'S 22-FOOT TALL STATUE WAS ACQUIRED BY FUTURE STUDIO OWNER AMY INOUYE WHO MOVED IT TO ITS CURRENT HOME IN 2007.

The Fremont Troll

Under the Aurora Bridge in Seattle lives a troll. This is no mythical being though, instead it's a giant sand sculpture and a work of modern art. The Fremont Troll appeared under the bridge that connects the Queen Anne and Fremont districts of the city in 1990, after winning the Fremont Arts Council's art competition the year before. The challenge was for artists to provide ideas on how to revitalise the area under the bridge that had become dangerous and in disrepair, frequented by fly tippers and drug dealers. The winning concept was for an 5.5 metre (18 feet) troll that riffed on the Three Billy Goat's Gruff fairy tale and the false reports of troll sightings under the bridge itself.

The sculpture was designed by a sculptor from the University of Washington along with two of his architecture students and his then-girlfriend. It then took a team of volunteers three months to build. It weighs 5,900kg (13,000lbs) and is constructed from a mesh of steel, wire and cement, allowing it to still stand tall 35 years after it was made.

The iconic troll is a magnet for family photo opportunities as children and adults are encouraged to clamber over it. It is sometimes

> ❝ The challenge was to revitalise the area under the bridge

decorated with different styles and garments. In the troll's right hand is a crushed Volkswagen Beetle, that the mythical being is intent on snacking on. The small iconic car initially contained a time capsule with Elvis memorabilia in, but this was sadly stolen by vandals, shortly after its construction. The troll has also been spray painted, infamously once with green fingers, tattoos, eyes and fangs. This resulted in the addition of more concrete to cover it up, making its skin even more bulbous. These occurrences necessitated the installation of floodlights to help prevent further damage and the sculpture remains a popular tourist attraction by day and a partying spot by night.

Nearby is what is known as the Troll's Knoll Community Garden. Opened in 2016, it is a volunteer-maintained allotment, tool shed and park. Three of the plots even provide for the city's food banks. If there's a good time to pay the troll a visit, it's 'Trolloween' – the beast's very own birthday celebrations. Taking place, naturally, on Halloween (31 October), Trolloween boasts live music and a costumed procession called the Haunt of Fremont.

Location: Seattle, Washington
Time zone: UTC-8

TIP VISIT AT 'TROLLOWEEN' ON 31 OCTOBER TO ENJOY THE FESTIVITIES!

Fremont Troll

Sounding just like a fairy tale, underneath a bridge in Seattle lies a troll that, controverting its name, has made this area of the city more safe and fun

WORDS **Jack Griffiths**

Main The crushed Beetle, forever caged in concrete, used to be coloured red and has a California license plate

Over left Situated under the north end of the bridge, the famous troll has appeared in a number of films and even in a song

Left Trolloween is a big deal in Seattle. Held every Halloween, its performances and parades have pagan themes

THE LONELIEST

It may have an uninspiring nickname, but ghost towns and bleak beauty make Nevada's Route 50 a stunning drive

WORDS Jamie Frier

Austin Summit represents the halfway point of your journey and the start of one of the longest straight stretches of the route. Hello cruise control

Image Getty Images

Location
Carson City, Nevada
~
Time zone
UTC-8

Nevada, Route 50

ROAD IN AMERICA

Yes, it's called the Loneliest Road in America. No, this doesn't make you think it's a route you'd want to drive unless you really aren't a people person. However, Route 50, which cuts straight through the heart of Nevada, is one of the most unique road trips you'll take. Abandoned ghost towns, dramatic landscapes and sandboarding make this lonely road one you'll want to tell all your friends about.

TIP
GET A STAMP AT FIVE OF THE EIGHT MAJOR TOWNS ON ROUTE TO EARN AN "I SURVIVED" BADGE.

Fairview Mountain offers exactly what its name suggests. A fair view of the Nevada countryside

> " US-50 is a heady mix of mountainous terrain, stark plains and natural sights

The backstory behind the name is simple. In 1986, an American Automobile Association (AAA) rep described Route 50 in *Life* magazine, saying; "It's totally empty. There are no points of interest. We don't recommend it. We warn all motorists not to drive there unless they're confident of their survival skills." But nearly 40 years on, this statement doesn't hold up as the Nevadans have leaned into this by creating a feature of the country's loneliest road.

US-50 starts in Sacramento, California, and continues to the Atlantic Coast. But the part you're concerned with begins and ends in Nevada - one of the US's least-densely populated states. The road trip can be enjoyed in either direction, but on this trip you'll be travelling from Carson City on the western edge of Nevada to Baker, just outside the Great Basin National Park on its eastern border.

Having gambled to your heart's content in Reno, drive south on the 580 before turning left at Carson City onto US-50. It isn't long before you hit Dayton, the place where gold was first discovered in Nevada. It's a medium-sized town with everything you could need, from fuel to restaurants to, naturally, casinos. Passing through Dayton, it isn't long before you begin to understand what that AAA rep meant. The bustling town is gone almost as soon as it appeared, leaving you gazing at a sparse, bleak and unkempt landscape on both sides of the highway. In the distance are mountains, but they, like everything else, seem an incredibly long way away.

Continue east, taking a right fork down to Fallon. The mountains have all but disappeared with nothing but the occasional gas station or industrial building for company. Cross over Carson River and enter Fallon - one of the bigger towns on your journey, so a good place to stop for some food and a freshen up. If you want to push on through, then again you'll quickly be into some seriously open territory, but at least on this occasion there are signs of life with crop fields reaching far away on either side. Occasionally quaint little wooden houses line the roadside, proving that there is indeed life to be found if you look hard enough. On the whole though, it is a barren landscape, oddly beautiful with the only human-made things in sight being telephone poles and the road itself. Crops make way for sand and shrubs, while the distant mountains edge ever nearer. Resourceful Nevadans have found a way to make use of the area's natural resources with the Sand Mountain Recreation Area. The mountain itself is five kilometres (three miles) long, 1.6 kilometres (one mile) wide and 180 metres (600 feet) tall and is the largest single dune in the Great Basin area. You will have to pay to enter but it gives you the chance to ride ATVs and sandboards over the dunes, while naturalists can hunt for the Sand Mountain blue butterfly. There is also a Pony Express station from 1860 for those who want a history fix. Just make sure to take plenty of water, as there isn't any available in the area.

Back onto the road and the mountains draw ever closer, some hugging the side of the road as you cut through the rising hills on either side, feeling suddenly claustrophobic after the wide expanses you have been used to. However, after heading through Sand Springs Pass, the road opens out again and your perception is flipped on its head as the slight decline shows the road stretching out far into the distance. If you need a stop, Fairview and Wonder are abandoned Gold Rush towns, but only the latter is accessible. Fairview Mountain, however, is certainly worth a visit. Turn right off the highway and to the base of the mountain. Two-wheel-drive cars can't make it very far, but four-wheel-drive vehicles can get a reasonable way up before you hike the rest of the way to the summit for great views of the Nevada plains.

One quirky place to take a rest is the Shoe Tree. Legend has it that a newly married couple got into an argument and the husband threw

Nevada, Route 50

the wife's shoes into a tree. They reconciled and an icon was born, with locals and tourists hurling their footwear into the branches. Sadly the tree was cut down illegally in 2010, but in 2017 a new tree was designated the Shoe Tree. It's been gaining soles and souls ever since.

The road twists and winds as it continues east until you hit the town of Austin, which is around 275 kilometres (175 miles) from the start of your journey. It's a good place to fill up with fuel, food and bed down for the night, given that it's roughly halfway through the route.

Once through Austin, the route starts to twist and climb, affording excellent places to stop and take in all the wondrous nothingness that Nevada has to offer. There's something truly peaceful about gazing out into an untouched landscape, and Nevada has this in spades. As you wind into the sandy hills that loom up either side of the road, you could be forgiven for thinking you had accidentally slipped into Arrakis from *Dune*, such is the otherworldly vibe they give off. About five kilometres (three miles) outside of Austin you'll reach Austin Summit and begin your descent through sweeping curves back towards sea level and some kind of greenery. It's still a further 100 kilometres (62 miles) from here to the next town and around half of that is along a gun-barrel-straight stretch of tarmac that seemingly has no end in sight. For this part of the road trip it's all about the cruise control, good tunes and good chat to keep those miles ticking over.

Gorgeous as the open road is, it's something of a relief when you finally hit the next town of Eureka – a particularly apt name if you're looking for gas, a rest stop, some food or just another human! This place is true rural America, with hardware stores, roadside cafes, painted wooden houses with white picket fences and a sign declaring it to be the friendliest town on the loneliest road in America, which doesn't seem like a huge boast! After a well-earned break, continue south through more mountainous terrain, before the road sweeps east and you hit another never-ending ribbon or road. This time it's 125 kilometres (78 miles) until the next town with only a handful of bends to stop you dropping off the edge of the Earth. Ely is that next town and it is chock full of nods to its past as a mining town, with ghost towns, old-fashioned railways and museums galore. Your route will cut south and then eastwards again until you reach Baker and the pinnacle of your trip – the Grand Basin National Park. This is an absolutely stunning area of natural beauty, resplendent with mountains, trails, caves and ancient trees, including the bristlecone pine, which, at over 5,000 years old, is the world's oldest living organism.

So far from being the Loneliest Road in America, US-50 is instead a heady mix of mountainous terrain, stark plains, friendly villages, ghost towns, natural sights and human-made thrills. If this is someone's idea of lonely, imagine what their idea of busy is! ★

AN OASIS IN THE DESERT

Shortly after leaving Dayton, your route east will take you through a number of tiny towns before a surprise appears. Looming up out of nowhere on your right-hand side is a body of water, so unexpected, flat and still you could be forgiven for believing it's a mirage. However, it's no figment of the imagination, rather Lahontan Reservoir, a vast human-made water source tapped from Carson River thanks to a huge dam. Surrounding the reservoir are beaches, camping sites and locals enjoying fishing and watersports. You might only be around 70km (43mi) into your trip, but if it's a hot Nevadan summer's day, the reservoir could prove to be a welcome relief from the heat. You can also see the few ruined remains of Lahontan City, which was once home to hundreds of workers who built the dam and stayed on site rather than commute from nearby towns. The city was a bustling, lively place but was quickly abandoned following the dam's completion in 1915. Now all that is pretty much gone, save for a handful of ruined buildings, rubble and pottery.

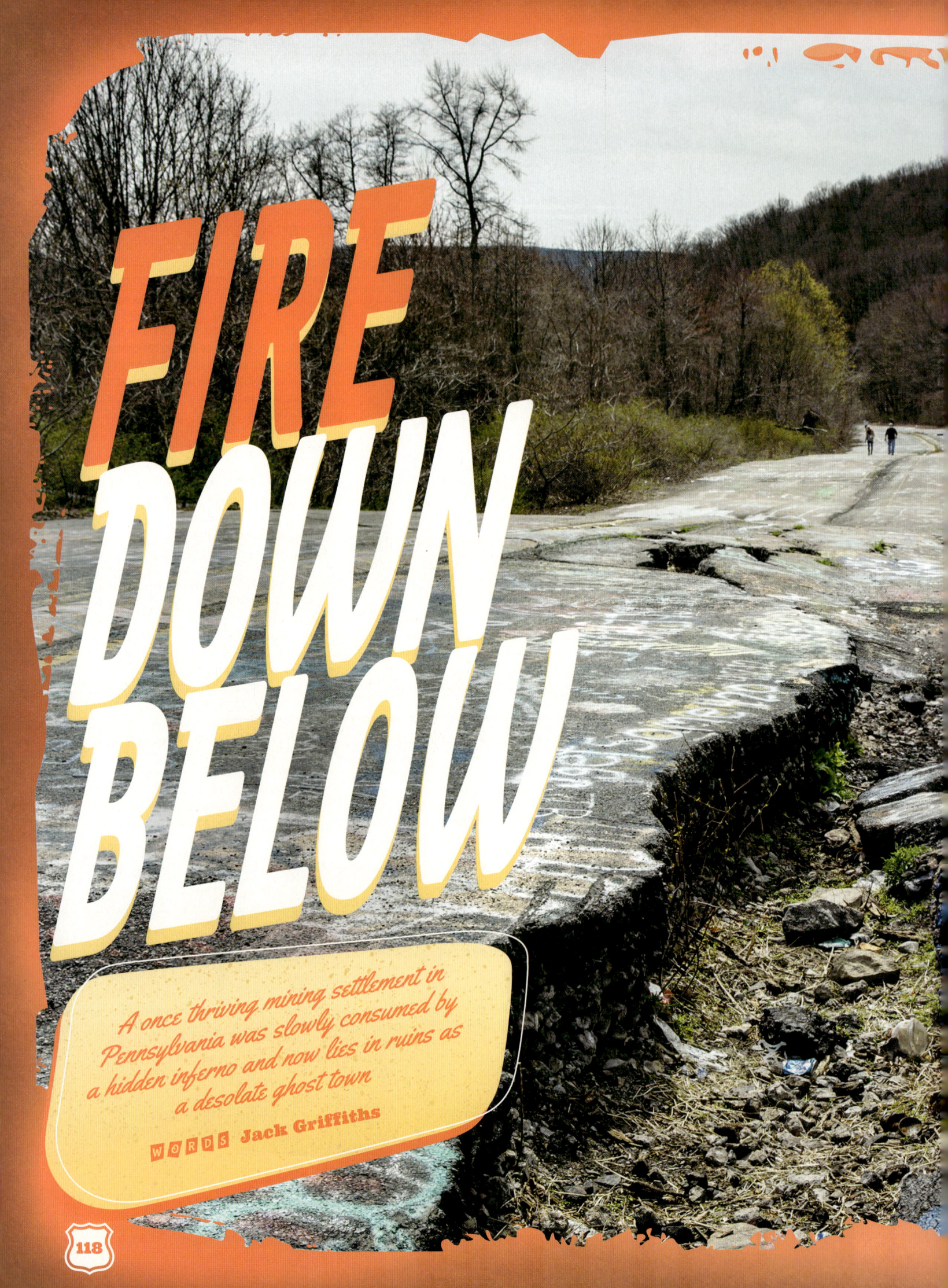

FIRE DOWN BELOW

A once thriving mining settlement in Pennsylvania was slowly consumed by a hidden inferno and now lies in ruins as a desolate ghost town

WORDS **Jack Griffiths**

Centralia

Centralia was a simple mining town in Northeastern Pennsylvania before its history changed forever on Valentine's Day 1981. That morning, the ground suddenly opened up beneath the feet of residents, revealing an underground blaze that would engulf the town whole.

The coal-rich Centralia had been a popular mining area since the 1850s with no less than 14 mines. It had started to decline a century later as oil and gas became the preferred energy sources. As industry relocated, what remained was a network of tunnels and coal seams. The area was so vast that a subterranean fire went unnoticed. Believed to have ignited in 1962, it was fed by the storing and subsequent controlled burning of the town's landfill, as well as the coal in the mines, and was unbeknownst to the locals.

What was just a few embers became a blaze that spread slowly but surely through the remaining coal. Still hidden underground, it was only noticed months afterwards when smoke finally started to appear and the smell of sulphur filled the air. When people began to faint in their homes due to carbon monoxide poisoning and trees began to die, it was time to act. What followed was years of attempts to try to extinguish the fire but to no avail, with the plentiful coal acting as an almost-infinite fuel supply. As the threat remained, many locals left the town, wary of potential disasters like the one that was to occur in February 1981, when the relentless fire caused the ground to collapse in on itself.

Following the sinkhole incident, funding was provided by authorities to re-house former residents and only a select few remained in Centralia, which became a near-ghost town In 2002 its ZIP code was removed following rerouting of the highway. Many of the houses have been demolished and overgrown vines cling to abandoned homes as funding has dwindled and state interest has decreased. Despite all this, some people remain and the town continued to have a council, a mayor and even a weekly newspaper. The remaining handful of residents had to fight a legal battle with the state to maintain their ownership over their properties and it is likely the government will take full control of the area once these people are gone.

The fire continues to burn and will do so for many more years. Access to Centralia is heavily restricted with almost all roads to and from the town blocked or in disrepair. ★

Main Centralia was abandoned, as were the roads leading to it. Graffiti Highway, a section of Route 61, is in complete disrepair

Below left A few remain in Centralia but the continued threat of the fire beneath it means the area is consigned to being deserted

Below Smoke continues to rise, with the fire still burning below the ground and showing no signs of stopping any time soon

Location
Centralia, Pennsylvania
~
Time zone
UTC-5

What Really Happened in

The name Roswell will already be familiar to many readers, especially fans of science fiction, who may well have enjoyed three whole seasons of the popular television series of the same name, followed by a later spin off. Both of these shows were influenced by a mysterious incident in 1947 that sparked not only a cultural movement and litany of alien-related fiction, but countless conspiracy theories the world over.

Located in southeastern New Mexico, until the early 1940s Roswell was known for its agriculture and ranching. In 1941 it became a centre of military activity when the Walker Air Force Base was established, a development that significantly boosted the local economy. Perhaps that's all it would have been synonymous with were it not for a peculiar event six years later that would change the fate of Roswell and its inhabitants forever.

A few weeks prior to the night that would transform life in Roswell, a bizarre sighting over 2400 kilometres (1500 miles) to the north drew widespread media attention. At around 3pm on the afternoon of 24 June 1947, pilot Kenneth Arnold was assisting in the search for a downed military aircraft over the Cascade Mountains, Washington State, when on turning eastward he observed nine crescent-shaped objects flying in echelon formation (like geese) at an approximate height of 3000 metres (9800 feet) and travelling at supersonic speed. He described seeing "a bright flashing light, similar to sunlight reflecting from a mirror" and the movement of these unidentified flying objects as being jerky and "like a saucer would (move) if you skipped it over water". Incidentally, this is where the phrase 'flying saucer' comes from - and it kicked off a widespread 'flying saucer craze' across the USA.

While there had been reports of strange aerial phenomena across the US prior to Arnold's unsettling experience (during WWII, Allied pilots had reported seeing glowing balls of light they called 'foo fighters', which were also spotted over large parts of Europe), there had been no official sightings in Roswell. Understandably, news of Arnold's claims caused great interest and speculation across the country, including among the residents of Roswell. Some believed similar sightings to have been commonplace, while others queried why they had not been

Location
Chaves County, New Mexico
~
Time zone
UTC-7

Roswell?

Roswell, New Mexico

The US Government remains adamant that the aircraft that crashed in New Mexico was made by humans, but there are many who claim it was not of this world

WORDS Bee Ginger

reported, or if they had, then was there more to the story? They had no idea that their city was about to be thrust into the UFO limelight.

In the first week of July (the precise date is still debated), reports of an extraterrestrial spacecraft crashing at speed in the vast and arid desert of Lincoln County, New Mexico, started to circulate. Mysterious debris, and possibly even the remains of the alien crew, were said to have fallen from the sky, scattering across the Brazel Ranch not far from Roswell.

Initially, WW "Mac" Brazel, the owner of the ranch, didn't think too much of the fragments he'd found.

Unaware of the Washington incident (and subsequent sightings elsewhere), he gathered what appeared to be shards of a metallic substance and stored them. However, when he later heard rumours of flying saucers and spaceships in the area, he notified a sheriff in Roswell, who in turn informed the relevant authorities, including the personnel from the nearby army base.

Major Jesse Marcel and Captain Sheridan Cavitt were dispatched by Rosewell Army Air Field (RAAF) to accompany Brazel to the crash site in order to recover more of the debris so it could be taken by the US Government and thoroughly examined. A statement prepared by local journalist Walter Haut and the base's public information officer followed and was released on Newswire (a valuable tool used to alert media outlets of up-to-date and breaking news that can then be used to broadcast to a wider audience). The Newswire transcript stated the following:

"The many rumours regarding the flying disc became a reality yesterday when the intelligence office of the 509th Bomb Group of the Eighth Air Force, Roswell Army Air Field, was fortunate enough to gain possession of a disc through the cooperation of one of the »

121

TIP
ROSWELL IS BEST VISITED IN SPRING OR FALL, WHEN THE TEMPERATURES ARE MILDER AND THE CITY ISN'T CROWDED WITH FESTIVAL GOERS.

local ranchers and the sheriff's office of Chaves County. The flying object landed on a ranch near Roswell sometime last week. Not having phone facilities, the rancher stored the disc until such time as he was able to contact the sheriff's office, who in turn notified Major Jesse A Marcel of the 509th Bomb Group Intelligence Office.

"Action was immediately taken and the disc was picked up at the rancher's home. It was inspected at the Roswell Army Air Field and subsequently loaned by Major Marcel to higher headquarters."

The world drew a collective breath of shock at the news and awaited updates, which soon came in the form of a complete reversal from the US military less than 24 hours later. The new statement reported that a mistake had been made and that the debris was in fact from a wayward weather balloon.

Newspapers printed the update complete with a series of photographs taken at the headquarters in Fort Worth (where the debris had been transported to) of Marcel, General Roger Ramey and other military personnel examining debris that looked similar to the tinfoil you would use to wrap a sandwich. The explanation of the weather balloon was widely believed: social media and 24-hour news didn't exist yet, and conspiracy theorists remained in the minority. People simply believed what they were told. In time the newspapers became tomorrow's trash, and as the ink faded so too did the memory of the extraterrestrial 'visitation'. But it wasn't to remain buried forever.

In 1978, the incident in Roswell resurfaced when shocking information was leaked to the media by a whistleblower involved in the original operation. The weather balloon story was said to have been a cover up, with photos of the wreckage from the balloon carefully staged. The extraterrestrial spacecraft had existed and been taken away for intensive investigation at Area 51, a highly classified US Air Force facility in the south of Nevada. Witnesses and anyone connected to the incident and findings were sworn to silence.

A number of eyewitnesses were subsequently tracked down and questioned by researchers. They corroborated the flying saucer story, stating that it had indeed been retrieved and that the deceased bodies of the spacecraft's

> *People started to question the official narrative and whether there was a cover up*

crew were also removed and subjected to autopsies. Workers at the morgue in Roswell told researchers of a truck arriving with armed guards, who proceeded to offload the small bodies of otherworldly creatures before whisking them into the building. Technicians from the US military were even reported to have reverse-engineered the spaceship.

The court of public opinion had changed over the years following the war in Vietnam and the assassination of President John F Kennedy, and trust in the government was at an all time low. People started to question the official narrative and whether in fact there had been a cover up. Researchers even interviewed Jesse Marcel again, who told them of intimidation tactics and threats being used against anyone suspected of speaking out about what really happened. The phrase 'bullets are cheap' was regularly used, and many feared they would be silenced indefinitely if they spoke up or corrected the narrative. So who was telling the truth? The

Roswell, New Mexico

DESERT DAY TRIP

Top left A copy of the Roswell Dispatch newspaper which claimed the findings were from a weather balloon

Middle left Major Jesse Marcel at Fort Worth, Texas, holding tinfoil-like pieces of debris originally reported to come from an extraterrestrial spaceship

Far left Roswell's iconic branch of McDonald's is shaped like a UFO with glowing neon lights

Above The 1947 crash landing actually took place around 112 kilometres (70 miles) north of Roswell

US Government, or the numerous witnesses who were adamant they'd been warned to keep quiet? There seemed to be no conclusive answer either way.

It wasn't until many years later, in 1994, that the US Congress opened an official investigation into the Roswell incident. This concluded that there was a perfectly human explanation behind the crash. In 1947 the Cold War had been in its infancy, and the US harboured concerns that the Soviet Union was conducting nuclear bomb tests. In response Project Mogul, a top-secret operation, was launched by the CIA and US Navy during 1947 just 240 kilometres (150 miles) to the west of Roswell at the Alamogordo Army Air Field.

Large balloons would be sent up into the sky with a small gondola-shaped boat underneath them containing a radiosonde (a battery-powered telemetry device) and cameras inside in order to track the balloons as they rode the jet stream across the Atlantic in search of Soviet nuclear test sites. It is believed that one of these balloons crashed all those years ago on the Brazel Ranch, as in addition to the tinfoil, balsa wood and metal strips were also uncovered among the detritus.

Another report from the US Air Force followed in 1997 regarding the 'bodies' discovered in the wreckage. Apparently, as part of a later top-secret investigation, tests were conducted to "assess the effects on the human body in the case of a pilot being ejected from an aircraft and falling to the ground from a high altitude". This was achieved by throwing crash test dummies out of an aircraft over the desert, thereby accounting for the supposedly alien corpses. Any previous sightings of extraterrestrial beings were attributed to false memories.

What really happened in Roswell will probably be debated and questioned forever more, the incident just one of many events shrouded in mystery that conspiracy theorists point to as evidence of a government cover up. Regardless of what the facts actually are, its legend remains firmly ensconced in UFO lore, cementing Roswell in the minds of alien enthusiasts as a must-see destination. Perhaps those searching for proof of an extraterrestrial collision will one day find the evidence many believe has been hidden for almost 80 years. Or maybe, on this occasion, the truth of what the US authorities were really up to was just as strange as the fiction. ★

The Roswell incident has of course become a huge draw to the area, transforming the main street of Roswell into an epicentre for alien enthusiasts. There are lampposts and letter boxes adorned with alien symbolism, and a great number of souvenir shops and eateries that honour the theme. Even the local McDonald's is shaped like a UFO, which at nighttime burns bright with neon lights. The menu is rumoured to be out of this world.

If the International UFO Museum and Research Center located on Main Street is not your cup of tea then there are plenty of other, more-down-to-earth activities to be enjoyed. For lovers of contemporary art, the Anderson Museum of Contemporary Art is well worth a visit (www.rair.org/about-amoca). There are also galleries dotted around the centre featuring unique works by local artists.

The area also boasts a number of parks ideal for trekking, cycling and water sports. Bottomless Lakes State Park is particularly good for scuba diving, as the lakes were formed by sinkholes that are around 27 metres (90 feet) deep.

The Bitter Lake National Wildlife Refuge is a haven for photographers, as the area is protected and provides habitat for some of the region's most unique and rare animals and birdlife (no alien sightings have yet been reported). For further information see **www.seeroswell.com**.

AREA 51

In Nevada, the mysterious government facility known as Area 51 looms menacingly over the desert. Could there really be aliens behind the barbed wire?

WORDS Catherine Curzon

At nearly 100 miles long, the remote Nevada State Route 375 is so celebrated for its frequent UFO sightings that in 1996, Nevada officially classed it as the Extraterrestrial Highway. The highway is open to the public but one place that definitely isn't is Area 51, a highly classified United States Air Force (USAF) facility that lies close to the highway and is considered by many to be the epicentre of extraterrestrial activity in the United States. Whilst visitors are not permitted at Area 51, it continues to exert a pull over conspiracy theorists, UFO-watchers and lovers of all things weird.

Though Area 51 is under the administration of Edwards Air Force Base, its research and work is so top secret that the CIA did not even admit to its existence until 2013. To this day it remains a place shrouded in secrecy and has become legendary as a byword for dark and mysterious government deeds.

Perhaps the most well-known theory regarding Area 51 is that it is where alien technology is stored by the government. Depending on who is telling the tale this ranges from anything from the debris from crashed UFOs, to operational alien spacecraft and even the remains of dead aliens or live extraterrestrial beings. At the centre of this theory sits the infamous Roswell Incident, which many people still believe marks the moment aliens landed on earth, albeit unintentionally.

On 8th July 1947, the USAF issued a brief press release in which they announced that they had recovered what they called a flying disc from a ranch near Roswell, New Mexico. The wreckage had been found on the land of a rancher named William "Mac" Brazel, who called in his discovery. However, no sooner had the press release appeared than it was superseded by a second statement,

Opposite Known as the Extraterrestrial Highway, Nevada State Route 375 is the heart of American UFO culture, with sightings reported frequently

Right Area 51 is very definitely not open to the public, but many believe it's home to aliens and extraterrestrial technology

Images Getty Images

Area 51, Nevada

Location
Groom Lake, Nevada
~
Time zone
UTC-8

Above left One place you can be sure of a welcome is the Little A'Le'Inn

Above Journalist George Knapp has done much to publicise Area 51, helping it to achieve its near-legendary status amongst conspiracy theorists

Above right The Aurora is a spy plane that some believe was engineered using alien technology; the US government denies that it ever existed at all

> *The rumour mill went into overdrive and rumours spread of a crashed UFO*

in which officials explained that the flying disc was actually the remains of a crashed weather balloon. This should have been the end of the matter but instead the rumour mill went into overdrive and rumours spread of a crashed UFO, with its remains and those of its crew being bundled off to Roswell Air Force Base for experimentation.

Area 51 entered the story in 1989 when a man named Bob Lazar gave an anonymous interview to a Las Vegas television host named Bill Knapp, who perhaps did more than most to fuel the flames of Area 51 conspiracies. In the broadcast, he claimed to have been an employee at Area 51. Lazar claimed to have been one of a team who was employed to reverse engineer one of nine flying saucers kept at the base, all of which he alleged had come from beyond the stars. Lazar's claims led to speculation amongst the UFO community that the crashed craft from Roswell was held at Area 51 and that it was this, which Lazar dubbed "the sport model", on which he had been working. Lazar's story was a sensation and sparked the interest in Area 51 which has since refused to die. Though it has been pointed out that he offered no physical proof and that his credentials are questionable, Lazar's supports point out that it is in the interest of the government to discredit him and to make him seem like a fraud.

Because of the immense level of security clearance required to work at Area 51, employees are unable to discuss their work and anyone who claims to have been an employee and must therefore remain anonymous is immediately open to suspicion when it comes to their veracity. For some, this explains why the government claim that Bob Lazar was never an employee whilst to others, it is proof that he is a fraud.

Yet it is Lazar's story that has really struck a chord with the public. To this day, Area 51 is regarded as the place in which high level scientists and researchers have access to alien technology. Here, if the conspiracy theorists are to be believed, the US government is reverse engineering alien technology in order to recreate and harness it for their own ends. A documentary in 1996 featured claims that engineers had built a flying disc simulator that was used to train pilots, read for when they took the controls of craft based on those seized. Supposedly, multiple spacecraft of various sorts are now held at Area 51 for this purpose, alongside extraterrestrial remains that are also being studied by researchers.

It was here at Area 51 that the sinister group known as Majestic 12 supposedly carried out much of their work. Though officially dismissed as a hoax, Majestic 12 was claimed to be a secret committee of military leaders, scientists, and government officials, assembled in 1947 by President Harry S Truman specifically to recover and carry out research into alien spacecraft. Intriguingly, though the US government rejected the Majestic 12 papers as a hoax, little has done to identify who created the apparently fraudulent collection of government reports, letters and more. For some, this is proof that the hoax might have been perpetrated by the government itself, hoping to throw people off the scent of the real remains of craft and aliens at Area 51 by introducing deliberate disinformation into the UFO community.

For some though, the extraterrestrials at Area 51 are anything but deceased. George Knapp, the journalist who interviewed Bob Lazar, later claimed that an unnamed source had told him that there was a live alien at Area 51. This alien, according to the source, was able to speak with researchers and had been recorded on a videotape which would

Area 51, Nevada

TIP
RACHEL, NEVADA HAS A COLD DESERT CLIMATE: IF YOU GO IN WINTER, DRESS FOR IT!

carried out on concentration camp victims, Mengele supposedly began a programme of experimentation to create an army of child-size aviators who would be landed in America to create a *War of the Worlds*-like hysteria. These were the bodies found at Roswell and taken to Area 51, claimed Jacobsen in 2011, to applause from some and derision from others. Amongst those who disbelieved this theory was George Knapp, who still believes that there are aliens at Area 51.

According to a documentary entitled *Dreamland* made in 1996, Area 51 is buzzing with aliens, both dead and alive. He interviewed a retired employee who claimed to have worked with an alien being named J-Rod, who was able to telepathically communicate with researchers. J-Rod also appeared in reports by a man named Dan Crain who claimed to have once been based at Area 51, where he was working alongside the alien with the aim of cloning alien viruses. These viruses would, according to Area 51 fans, be used as biological weapons. Like Bob Lazar, Dan Crain has found his credentials and claims under heavy scrutiny and doubt; also like Lazar, the accuracy of his disclosures has been disputed at length.

Whilst extraterrestrial beings and technology are certainly the backbone of the Area 51 myth, they are not the only strange things that conspiracy theorists believe are going on in the Nevada desert. In this arid landscape, some say, government researchers have been experimenting with a weather modification technique known as cloud seeding, in which chemicals are dispersed into the air in order to change the amount of precipitation. Whilst this is a real scientific technique, conspiracy theorists have focused on it as a means of governments being able to induce floods and disasters, or influence global warming, droughts and more. At Area 51, critics believe, cloud seeding has been expanded into the creation of hurricanes and other ruinous weather events, which can be used as weapons against their opponents.

Alongside teams of scientists working on weather modification, Area 51 followers claim that such sci-fi concepts as time travel and experimental, all-powerful laser weapons are the subject of experiments at the isolated Area 51 base. Many of these are supposedly based on the alien technology recovered from captured spacecraft and their crew and, of course, all are rejected out of hand by anyone remotely close to the government.

Whilst the thought of UFOs are testament to alien engineering skills, it is human engineers who supposedly built a vast underground rail system that criss-crosses the entire North American continent. Tales of the railway appear to have been born out of a nuclear research facility first mentioned in the *LA Times* in 2014. The facility was based in underground chambers just outside Area 51 and was connected by an overground railroad, which allowed for transport of materials to each part of the site. A small railroad, no doubt the one which connected the facilities, can

be released after the death of the source. However, following a congressional enquiry, Knapp claims that his source changed his story altogether and that his new version of events provided the background for yet another take on Area 51, this time by author Annie Jacobsen.

In a book published in 2011, Jacobsen used the information Knapp's source had given her to reject the theory of aliens altogether. Instead, she claimed that the craft which crashed at Roswell and was taken to Area 51 was actually piloted by humans. According to Jacobsen, Joseph Stalin spirited Nazi doctor Josef Mengele out of Germany and put him to work on a new project. Known as the "Angel of Death" for the experiments he

A VISIT TO RACHEL

With a population now just 48, the little town of Rachel in Lincoln County, Nevada, has achieved celebrity status as the closest settlement to Area 51. Situated along the Extraterrestrial Highway, Rachel has welcomed its mysterious neighbour's infamy with open arms and received many visitors every year, all of whom are keen to know more about Area 51. Tourists can check into the local motel before picking up some souvenirs at a gift shop which specialises in alien-style items, then enjoy a meal at the Little A'Le'Inn, which is dedicated to extraterrestrial-themed treats including Alien Amber Ales and an Alien Burger!

Rachel has appeared in documentaries and video games that focus on Area 51 and became part of *The X-Files* world in two-part episode *Dreamland*, itself another name for Area 51. In 1996, the producers of *Independence Day* made a gift to the town of a time capsule, which will be opened in 2050. Visitors to Rachel consist of everyone from intrigued tourists to seasoned UFO-watchers and at night they pour out into the desert to watch the skies in the hope of seeing mysterious lights or more. For anyone fascinated by Area 51, it is a must-see destination.

THE BLACK MAILBOX

Nevada State Route 375, better known as the Extraterrestrial Highway, runs through the Nevada desert and past Area 51. It is here that fans gather to peer into the night sky, hoping for a glimpse of a visitor from another planet. Before the sun sets, however, many will stop off at the Black Mailbox, an iconic destination along the highway.

The Black Mailbox was once simply a mailbox owned by rancher Steve Medlin. Medlin grew so tired of Area 51 enthusiasts meddling with his mail that he eventually erected a new personal mailbox nearer to home. Once he had done so, however, an unknown person put the Black Mailbox in the place where his had once stood. It is the only landmark on the other otherwise featureless stretch of highway.

The mailbox is decorated with graffiti and stickers and it has become a place for visitors to leave a message or a gift for their extraterrestrial neighbours. Some people leave a note, others a little trinket, and people will travel for miles just to post something into the mailbox which has come to mean so much to UFO enthusiasts.

be seen on maps from 1983. However, over the years this has grown into the myth of the American secret underground railway, which is apparently used exclusively for clandestine government purposes.

More secretive journeys are rumoured to begin not underground but overground at a disappearing airstrip known as the "Cheshire Airstrip", after Lewis Carroll's Cheshire Cat. This airstrip at Area 51 is supposedly based on alien technology and is invisible to the naked eye until water is sprayed onto its surface, at which point it appears as if out of nowhere. The story of the Cheshire Airstrip originated with an anonymous pilot who regularly flew a commercial route around Nevada. He claimed that fellow pilots had told him that they were occasionally called upon to make landings at Nellis Air Force Base Complex, of which Area 51 is a part.

The pilots were instructed to land on what appeared to be a patch of scrub desert but as they made their approach, sprinklers were turned on that revealed a camouflaged asphalt runway, which gave disembarking passengers access to buildings that looked like unremarkable hills. For critics, this story has several problems. Firstly, they question why commercial pilots would be making such trips; after all, wouldn't it make much more sense for the USAF to use Air Force planes to transport employees to such top-secret locations, which revealed obviously experimental technology? Secondly and perhaps more mundanely is the point that there are completely normal and very terrestrial landing strips already available at Nellis. It would therefore make no sense in that case to reveal the existence of the Cheshire Airstrip to outsiders at all. Of course, conspiracy theorists say that this is the whole point: by revealing their existence, sceptics immediately decry them as nothing but rumours and hoax.; as double bluffs go, it would certainly make sense.

For lovers of aviation legend, Area 51 is synonymous with the Aurora, an American spy plane that has existed as a rumour for 40 years. Though the US government has dismissed the Aurora programme as nothing but make-believe, fans of Area 51 stories believe that the truth is very different. According to a Pentagon official, Aurora was actually a name given to a stealth bomber design competition early in its development, and this has caused confusion and the mistaken belief that there was a second airplane in development, but conspiracy theorists reject this as yet more disinformation. Instead, they claim that Aurora was a US black project, namely a highly classified project that was never acknowledged to the public, possibly based on alien technology.

The story gathered speed in 1989 when an engineer saw a mysterious triangular aircraft refuelling from a Boeing KC-135 Stratotanker above the North Sea, accompanied by two F-111 fighters. When the British Defence Secretary, Tom King, was asked about the sighting, he denied all knowledge of such a programme, though admitted that it wouldn't be surprising if it did in fact exist. For some, this was as good as an acknowledgment that Aurora was

Below Area 51 isn't only a government research centre that finds itself at the centre of a storm of conspiracy theories; it's become part of American culture, from films to festivals

Middle right According to conspiracy theorists, the alien craft that is rumoured to have crashed at Roswell was taken to Area 51, along with the remains of its crew

Bottom right Known as the Extraterrestrial Highway, Route 375 is the heart of American UFO culture, with sightings reported frequently

Area 51, Nevada

> **"Nobody should ever attempt to visit Area 51 or breach the security there"**

real, and more sightings followed across the UK and in America. For residents of Nevada who count Area 51 as a neighbour, the Aurora is very real indeed. There have been reports of the airplane taking off in the dead of night and at least one man captured footage on video. However, he has refused to release the tape, citing national security: if the Aurora is indeed a spy plane, this particular Nevada resident has no wish to reveal its existence to the world.

Many mysterious craft have been seen over Area 51, some believed to be extraterrestrial, some if not all actually human. According to the US government, most sightings of UFOs in the 1950s and 1960s can be put down to Project Oxcart, which led to the creation of the Lockheed A-12, a spy plane that was the progenitor of the Blackbird reconnaissance aircraft, which made its debut flight at Area 51 in 1962. These planes certainly looked unlike anything else in the sky in this era and it's easy to see why they, like the stealth fighter, may have been mistaken for alien technology. Of course, some ufologists claim that they look alien in nature precisely because the technology that spawned them originated in a galaxy far, far away.

In 2014 a YouTuber and experienced hiker, Kenny Veach, disappeared in the region of Area 51 whilst investigating a place he had named M Cave. Veach said that this cave, shaped like the letter M, made his body vibrate as he drew near it and left him with an overriding sense of terror. He chronicled his visit to the cave on his YouTube channel, saying that it was nothing like he had ever seen before. The area was exceptionally difficult and hazardous to explore, with abandoned mineshafts, some of which were used for chemical disposal, as well as rumours of drag activity and other hazards.

Many viewers believed Veach was a hoaxer whilst others asked him to go back and capture more footage. More sinister was a comment that warned him "don't go in, if you do, you won't get out", which was deleted soon after posting. On his first videotaped hike, Veach couldn't find the cave, leading to more accusations that the trip was a hoax. In reply Veach set out for another trip to the cave. He has not been seen since.

Veach's girlfriend believes he took his own life; others speculate that he met with an accident. For some, however, the disappearance of Kenny Veach is evidence that he found something he was not supposed to and was killed by the US military. To date, there is no explanation for his disappearance.

Area 51 is a functioning and fully operational US military facility and as such, it definitely isn't a place that welcomes tourists. Nobody should attempt to visit Area 51 nor breach the security there, but there are multiple attractions nearby that offer fans of all things extraterrestrial an experience to remember. The local area has embraced its reputation as the heartland of America's UFO culture and for visitors to Nevada, there is no end of ways in which they can delve into the mysteries of Area 51 without putting themselves at risk of arrest or perhaps worse. With shops, festivals and more devoted to the ever-fascinating Area 51, it has become an industry all of its own. So whilst Area 51 itself is very definitely out of bounds, if you find yourself on a dark night in the isolated Nevada desert, remember one thing: keep watching the skies. ★

DID YOU KNOW?!

ACCORDING TO THE DESIGNER OF THE LOCKHEED U-2, KELLY JOHNSON, AREA 51 WAS SELECTED BECAUSE OF THE NEARBY DRY LAKEBED, GROOM LAKE, WHICH MAKES A PERFECT NATURAL LANDING FIELD.

AMERICA'S WEIRDEST PLACES!

Future PLC Quay House, The Ambury, Bath, BA1 1UA

Bookazine Editorial
Editor **April Madden**
Art Editor **Thomas Parrett**
Head of Art & Design **Greg Whitaker**
Editorial Director **Jon White**
Managing Director **Grainne McKenna**

Contributors
Edoardo Albert, Rosie Cranie-Higgs, Catherine Curzon, Joanna Elphick, Jamie Frier, Ben Gazur, Bee Ginger, Jack Griffiths, Jessica Leggett, Alice Pattillo and Jon Wright

Cover images
Getty Images, Alamy, Shutterstock

All copyrights and trademarks are recognised and respected

Advertising
Media packs are available on request
Commercial Director **Clare Dove**

International
Head of Print Licensing **Rachel Shaw**
licensing@futurenet.com
www.futurecontenthub.com

Circulation
Head of Newstrade **Tim Mathers**

Production
Head of Production **Mark Constance**
Production Project Manager **Matthew Eglinton**
Advertising Production Manager **Joanne Crosby**
Digital Editions Controller **Jason Hudson**
Production Managers **Keely Miller, Nola Cokely, Vivienne Calvert, Fran Twentyman**

Printed in the UK

Distributed by Marketforce – www.marketforce.co.uk
For enquiries, please email: mfcommunications@futurenet.com

GPSR EU RP (for authorities only)
eucomply OÜ Pärnu mnt 139b-14 11317, Tallinn, Estonia
hello@eucompliancepartner.com, +3375690241

America's Weirdest Places First Edition (AHB7043)
© 2025 Future Publishing Limited

We are committed to only using magazine paper which is derived from responsibly managed, certified forestry and chlorine-free manufacture. The paper in this bookazine was sourced and produced from sustainable managed forests, conforming to strict environmental and socioeconomic standards.

All contents © 2025 Future Publishing Limited or published under licence. All rights reserved. No part of this magazine may be used, stored, transmitted or reproduced in any way without the prior written permission of the publisher. Future Publishing Limited (company number 2008885) is registered in England and Wales. Registered office: Quay House, The Ambury, Bath BA1 1UA. All information contained in this publication is for information only and is, as far as we are aware, correct at the time of going to press. Future cannot accept any responsibility for errors or inaccuracies in such information. You are advised to contact manufacturers and retailers directly with regard to the price of products/services referred to in this publication. Apps and websites mentioned in this publication are not under our control. We are not responsible for their contents or any other changes or updates to them. This magazine is fully independent and not affiliated in any way with the companies mentioned herein.

Future plc is a public company quoted on the London Stock Exchange (symbol: FUTR)
www.futureplc.com

Chief Executive Officer **Kevin Li Ying**
Non-Executive Chairman **Richard Huntingford**
Chief Financial Officer **Sharjeel Suleman**

Tel +44 (0)1225 442 244

Part of the

bookazine series